I0172760

Where Is Your Faith?

Where Is Your Faith?

Published and distributed in the United States by: Lulu.com

ISBN 978-0-6152-0366-9

I pray that this book will give you spiritual enlightenment for your mental ability to help build up your **faith** in Christ. This book is not intended to bash or damage anyone's belief, but it is designed to encourage those who sometimes feel hopeless and helpless in everyday situations. Throughout this book, you will learn that we all go through similar situations with different circumstances, which will give you recognition that we all have problems. I hope this book will help you learn how to deal with and what to accept in today's society, and also how to put your complete and total trust in **God**. God has used me to help generate a positive environment, and I pray that you will allow Him to use you to do the same.

This book is dedicated to my children, Ashley, Danielle, Celethea, Ra-maiya and Roman; all of whom **God** has given to me to help strengthen me as I travel my journey to become a better and stronger Christian. I love you all, and I hope this book helps you find everything you need to help strengthen your faith. I thank every human body and soul that seeks to make a change or a difference by taking the time to read this book and applying its contents to your life. Stay strong, stay grounded, and be **faithful**.

Chapter 1:
Jesus Is Our Lord and Savior

Hello, my name is Tonya Hardwick and I am a mother of five children; four girls and one boy. I am born to a mother of five children; four girls and one boy. My daughters are ages 20, 18, 17, & 10, and my son is 7. My mother's son Donald Gene Clark Jr., was the youngest after four girls as well; he is no longer with us as of 2003. My son means the "world" to me, just as my brother meant to my mother. I can only "imagine" the pain and agony of losing your only son. My son is special to me because he is symbolic to the love of **God** and His **Son** and what it must be like to give up your only son to save people who could care less about you or your son. As it is written in **Romans 8:3**, ***God*** sent His Son **Jesus** to **save us** so that we may have eternal life, forgiving us for "all" of "our sins" before we can even commit them. Written in **Matthew 1:21** it states that ***Jesus*** will be born to save us from sin. That's ***true love***! That's real love! That was a huge sacrifice to appear in human form to endure pain for a heap of people who are not even worthy of saving. Just imagine knowing that you are about to be tortured beyond unimaginable pain just to prove your unconditional love for someone. Stop and think about the sight of the pain ***Jesus*** felt from being struck on the head over and over again while others were spitting on Him and mocking Him about **His purpose for you**. What about the back pain He must have felt from having to carry the cross, and the burning sensation from the whips lashing against his skin? Imagine the feeling of the first nail that pierced His body, not just pin nails, but thick nails crushing the bones in His hands and tearing the flesh. It didn't stop at just His hands, but also the top of His feet, and to top it off they crowned His head with thorns. There were no respect and no regard for the sacrifice or the love He had for even the ones that were crucifying Him. Read that in **Matthew 27:28-40**. ***One*** "***Spirit***" came in human form and stood to take on all this cruel and unusual punishment just to prove His love for us so ***you and I*** could live an abundant life. Imagine going through all of that just to see happy feet and smiling faces. Why did they do this to Him? Because He came to share and spread the good news of the "***Word***" and show us how we can live an abundant life so we could **gain**

eternal life if we just follow Him. He came and showed us what true love and patience was all about, and how to care for each other with kindness. Never once did He ever do any physical or mental harm to any of His brothers and sisters in ***Christ***. **Jesus** came as **a spirit** in the form **of** human flesh created by **God**, the "***Ultimate Craftsman***," in His own image, with His breath planted inside of the seed before it even sprouted. This time came about when ***God*** saw the works of His first creations and how they caused grieve in his heart from how they turned out to be wicked and evil all the time. He had to wipe out the face of the earth with water. This fact is in **Genesis 6:5-7.** He wanted to do something different to create perfect peace and harmony. All of His thoughts were about "***US***" and how we can live a full and happy life. Even before planting the seed, **God made a sacrifice** to sit back and watch while His "only" Son was brutally murdered. ***God*** had US in mind with the knowledge of how painful and agonizing this death was going to be. Now, you ask yourself; for whom would you give up your only son or your only child for that matter? How many of us today would have the ***heart*** to make such a sacrifice? I don't see any of us being bold, loving, or caring enough to lend a helping hand much less give something away. **Remember, Jesus** after carefully considering the evilness of the world, "***chose***," to save us knowing that most of His death would be senseless and worthless because no one would trust or believe in Him, but He made the ***choice*** to do it anyway, taking in consideration of the ones that would make His death a worthy cost. This man loved us that much and we never even seen His face. Is your life even worth His death? What does ***Jesus*** really mean to you? Regardless of how you choose to view ***God's purpose*** for the world or what you have to say about how or why this all happened, the "fact" remains that it happened for "your" sake. There are so many unexplainable miracles and yet still no one "chooses" to ***believe***. This time the earth will be destroyed by fire which ***Hell*** will open up and consume **"*all*"** that belongs to it. This right here is the day and time to get your life right for your ticket through those ***Pearly Gates*** to your mansion. It is all based on your "**Faith**."

I can relate to ***God's pain*** from the way this world is today. He is just sitting back watching all this chaos and hatred in His creations. I can see the tears in His eyes as I write this explaining all of our evil ways and how we make His Son's death more and more worthless on a daily basis. Why is that not enough to make you want to **change your life** and your ways? It's right in front of your face every day, and if you **read the Bible** like you claim to do, your ways and attitudes should be a whole lot more different than what it is today. **We are** "all" brothers and sisters in **Christ**. What part of that phrase don't you understand? How can you claim ***love and unity*** when we are not all on the same page? ***God's creations*** and work should not be a game to you. He said, "**Come together as one in His name**." Check your characteristics and discard everything that is not ***Christ-like***. He created us to make a difference. You can see just how angry He is by all the devastation in this world. It doesn't have to be that way if we just stop living for ourselves instead of for ***Christ***. Let's reverse that and start ***living for Christ*** and not for ourselves. ***Jesus is Christ***. ***God*** told Satan that He would come back and destroy everything that ***Satan*** has corrupted. Honestly, if you think about it, ***God*** didn't intend for it to stay that way, but He knew that it would happen. He made a division between Heaven and Earth because He knew so many of us would let Satan take over our souls. Satan never appreciated the good works ***God*** had in store for us, so he set out to destroy them from the beginning. That's why he was kicked out of ***Heaven***. Satan didn't like that and felt that if he couldn't ***be in Heaven***, then he would set out to destroy everything good on earth. He already knew that everyone didn't **believe and trust in God;** those were the ones he already had. His mission was to get the ones who did trust and believe to turn their backs on ***God***. How can you stand to do that to ***God*** when He promised us so many good things if we just live for Him? When you **worship** and praise Him **in Spirit and in truth,** do it with love? **God is faithful** to all of His promises. Read about that in **Psalm 145:13**. Why can't we all just get along and accept each other in love? If you don't want to do it for anyone else, don't be so selfish, and do it for ***God***. **I love God** and if you claim the same, there should be proof behind your actions. When judgment day comes, and **it is** coming when you least expect it, you won't have a chance to say "I'm sorry" or make things right. **The time is now**.

Stop playing with ***God*** by using His name to portray to be something that you are not. He sees everything you do and hears everything you say. Instead of putting ourselves in everyone else's shoes, let's try putting them ***in God's***

hands. He does not listen to you when you come to Him and ask for forgiveness for mistreating other people when you know in your heart that you will do it again. No one can make you act a certain way. That is a "***choice***" you have made up in your mind by allowing ***Satan*** to take over. There is no real excuse for mistreating another human being for any reason at all when you are of **Christ**. We are to do what **Jesus** would do and make the best of any situation. What if you went to ***Jesus*** and asked Him to do something for you, or to give you something and He took a deep breath, told you "no," made a derogatory comment, or He just simply walked away from you. What would you say? Would it be something along the lines of "how and why would He do that to me?" Would you feel that because He is ***Jesus***, He is not supposed to be like that or act that way toward us? How would you feel? Hurt, disgusted, mistreated or mentally abused? ***Jesus*** loves us "in spite of." We would quickly remind ourselves and others of how ***Jesus*** should be. If this is the way you feel, and we are created in His image, then we should be the same way. Wouldn't you agree? I know most of you won't even ***acknowledge*** the things that I am speaking to you right now, but you can believe that you will answer to this message that is being delivered to your Spirit at this moment. He's going to ask you if you even attempted to, or considered making a change when He came crying and pouring His heart out to you about all of this sadness and wickedness in the world today. What will be your response? You won't be able to stand in front of Him and tell a lie because He will already know. What will you be able to testify for Him at that time? This life is not just about you, but what you are doing with it. Everything you do in this life "***will***" determine your punishment in the ***afterlife***. I speak and pour "my" heart out to you because I care, and it is important to me that ***we all*** get it right while we have the chance. It means everything to me and the world to ***God***, which by the way is His world and not ours.

Yes, it is true that this world is here for us to play in it, but it's mostly here for us to be more childlike minded and get along with everybody. That's why ***God*** doesn't hold "children" responsible for their actions, because they don't mistreat each other and they get along well with other children. When they see "adults" acting out and mistreating each other, they start to imitate them.

That is learned behavior for them; they are not born with it. Adults need to be adults and children need to be children and learn to respect each others title, but we can't get what we don't give. We are all to be a good loving example to each other. We don't have to go out the way we choose to. A lot of us are going through Hell and don't even see it. **Jesus is coming back** for His Father's children. Are you one of them? If you don't know Jesus, then He won't be coming back for you. Hear what I said, "If you don't **know Jesus**," not just ***God,*** you will be left here. Acknowledge the fact that ***God's*** "***Will***" is for you to know His Son. Once you get to know His Son and you believe His purpose, you can change your life. **Jesus is** the Spirit **in you**, so if you don't know and love "Him," you don't know and love yourself. You can't **seek God for direction** over your life until you get to know Jesus. To get direction, you must pray for ***knowledge*** and ***wisdom***, which will give you ***understanding***. You can't understand what you don't know. Understanding gives you strength, and strength gives you "**Faith**." It is better for you to **get to know God** and listen to His Son crying out inside of you, than it is for you to not know Him and go to Hell. You will surely suffer by lack of knowledge. People, we cannot use the excuse that we didn't **know** anything about **the Bible** and think that an excuse will get us in Heaven. Don't get His words confused for exception to His Kingdom. It is mentioned in the Bible about "**those who know me** will be with me." He gives "every" one of us the knowledge of how to seek His wisdom so we can understand our purpose. If you don't seek, how will you find? It is stated in the Bible that if ***Jesus*** never presents you to the Father, you don't stand a chance of making it in ***Heaven***. It is a "**Must**" that you know the Son. There is no exception. You can verify that in **John 14:6**. ***The Bible*** is available anywhere, and you hear ***God's Word*** just about everywhere you turn. **God** always **sends** someone your way that will speak about Him in some form or matter. Don't keep turning a deaf ear to the Father. Get to know more than just the name "***Jesus***." Just because you know His name that will not help you enter the Kingdom, especially when you continue to do evil works. You can verify that in **Matthew 7:21-23**. What you "seek" now is what you will "see" in the end. Will you see "love" or "hate?" Will you have eternal Life or Death? Are you headed for Heaven or Hell? It is ***your choice*** and your choice alone, so be wise about your decision.

What will it be?

Chapter 2:
My Purpose Is About Faith

I am here **speak**ing **to** you because **God** has called and ordered me to do this. I didn't question why, or go to anyone to seek advice to see if this was real. I just did it. I have learned from **Timothy I 4:13**, "Do not neglect your Gift." There is nothing anyone can do for me without the "good works of the Lord" above. I bring this to you because there is not enough of us standing up for ***Christ***. No one gave this revelation to me except ***God***, and I don't need anyone's permission or approval to do His work. I've made it up in my mind to live for ***Christ*** and surely for Him I will die. Many of you don't know me, but I am a child of ***God*** being used to reach out and touch your hearts and your souls so that you can feel ***God's pain*** crying out to you to seek Him for change. When ***God*** calls and tells you to do something, or He lays something on your heart to do, you don't ask "why?" Just do it. There is "***always***" a good reason when He calls. This is not of me speaking, but that of the **"**ONE**"** above. Besides, there is nothing I can say that you wouldn't be able to confirm throughout the ***Bible***, but it's totally up to you to verify that for yourself. Never let anyone tell you anything without going to verify the information given to you. What I'm sent to do is something that you are familiar with because you have heard this before. This kind of work for **the Lord will not stop** until the return of the "Almighty Himself." I am actually speaking to you to motivate you to **seek Christ** if you never have, and to **seek more** if you already have. Too often we sit back and do nothing when ***God*** is trying to move us. We are so stuck on ourselves with wanting this and wanting that, that we don't have enough time in "our" busy schedules to do what He has called or told us to do. **God is our future**, but we are so caught up thinking that we are advancing, but truthfully we're declining. We don't thank Him enough; whether it is for our first morning breath we take, the first breath after an afternoon nap, a long flight on the plane or bus, after falling asleep at our desks at work, or at the wheel of the car. There are so many things we have to be thankful for and forget every day to say it, not acknowledging the fact that in most of these cases, there are some people who just don't wake back up after these instances.

I have always wanted to know how I could reach out to people and motivate them to reach for a heart of goodness. I always felt that there was so much I wanted to say to people, but never knew how to reach that goal. I had to get myself together and build a better relationship with ***God*** so that I could get a feel for ***my purpose*** and know when He was speaking to me so I would know just what to do. I had to stop thinking about what can be done for me and start thinking about what I could do for others, and let ***God*** do what He is going to do for me. One thing I know for sure is that when I leave things up to ***God***, it's always going to work out for the best whether I see it or feel it at that time or not. "***NO***," things are not going to be easy doing it that way, but in the end it will all be well worth it. **God** never **promised** an easy life only because He already knew that we wouldn't "**Follow His Lead**, but He did promise us a good life in the end if we do follow." Some people would like to believe that life is hard, but that is only mind over matter. Life is what you make it; so if your life seems to be hard that is a ***choice*** of how you ***choose*** to live your life. However, you are the only one who can change it as long as you seek help from the good ***Lord*** above. Make the choice to live a good life and let it be a positive example of how easy it is to choose what goes and comes into your life. For whatever comes into your life that you plan to dispose of, make sure you send it off with something positive, and when you plan for something to stay give it a reason to want to be around. Remember one thing; you are equipped with the strength from ***God*** to stop doing anything you want to. The willpower lies in your strength, and you can only utilize it when you recognize that fact by simply making the choice to stop and sticking with it. The choice only becomes difficult when we make an excuse for why we should keep doing that thing that we keep "***claiming***" we want to stop. Once you put "claim" on something it's already done when you start "believing" in it. Everything we do is mind over matter and we need to stop making excuses for why we want to continue doing things that we know are wrong. Until we stop using the excuse that we are human/flesh as an excuse to do wrong, we will never be able to make a change for something good. The more we keep "claiming" to be flesh, the more we will allow ourselves to continue lying, cheating, stealing, killing and blaming ***God*** for our downfalls and mistakes. ***Choose*** the life you want to live today and set standards for what you will and will not accept, and don't let anything or anyone stand in your way that is outside of ***Christ***. Don't let others get you upset and turn you away from them because that only makes you just like them, which is what they want. When you let someone upset you, you give them the victory. When you are taking your Christian walk, don't let anyone tell you that you are phony, that it is too late for you, or it will never work for you. It only takes as long as you allow it to. If someone tries to discourage you in any kind of manner, without getting upset, you let them know that you will pray for them. They are only being represented by ***Satan***. Have a made-up mind to **serve God** and no one else. When I had it made up in my mind that I wanted to change things by striving to live for ***Christ***, I started to see and hear things more clearly. ***God*** gave me revelation of what I'm speaking today. I don't know what ***God*** has in store for me, but I know I want to do my part in spreading the "***Word,***" which is about ***Jesus***. So however I feel led, that's what I'm going to do. **My purpose** is to have total **faith**, **dedication**, and **love for Christ**. I know it's not going to be easy, but if I want it bad enough, which I do, it will work. For whatever it is I am sent to do, I thank ***God*** for using me.

My purpose here is to help you see and understand what the "***sin***" you are committing is doing to ***God***. This is in no way, form, shape, or matter being brought to you to convict you as a person because ***God*** will always love you "in spite of," but it is to help you understand that your "actions" are delaying the promises that ***God*** has for you. It is not you as a person that the problem lies within, but it is within your actions that cause people to judge you. ***God*** wants to use us for something positive, but in order for Him to do that we must be in the right Spirit. ***God*** has plans for your life and with or without your cooperation; they will come to past as planned. I just pray that you are still here to be a part of them. I am not here to judge you because that is not my job and I don't know your purpose or the reasons of why you do the things you do. I'm **com**ing **to** you because **God** is tired of His **"*saints*"** not being serious about His business. We are all supposed to be His "***Faithful***" servants? We claim to be "**Christians**," but our hearts and characteristics show otherwise. Our **work for the Lord** is never done; it continues until the day of our last breath. If you are a true servant, then ***serve***. He didn't give us any limitations for our work of service; we limit them ourselves. His work is to be done outside of the ***Church*** as well as inside. It's bad when people leave the church and don't come back. That is an indication that we are pushing someone away, because they don't feel like they are in the presence of the ***Lord***. If you are a "***true Saint***," anyone that comes around you should automatically feel and see something different about you. They should recognize a certain glow about you. They should see true happiness written all over your face. Your presence should make them want to be more like you. You may beg to differ, but that is what a "***true saint***" would represent.

I'm here to **speak the truth** about how to truly **be a Christian**. I'm here to present this to you because we are destroying ***God's*** whole ***purpose*** for our life. Why do we look people up and down when they come into the church, give terminal steers, and whisper? How can anyone feel comfortable walking in the house of the ***Lord***, if the "***wanna***" be ***Saints*** in there are the first ones to show outsiders that church is not what Saints claim it to be? First of all, we go to church to hear the "***Word***" so the sick can be healed and delivered from their sins. If you are so much filled with the ***Holy Spirit*** and you see something wrong with the way someone may be approaching the church, then that is your responsibility or your duty to go **show** them **love and support** and take them to the side and ***pray*** with them, and let them know that ***God*** will work it out if they so truly desire. The **Saints** in the churches are the ones keeping the lost out. They know that the biggest hypocrites are the ones in the Churches. The **Church is** supposed to be **"One body" of Christ**; a whole congregation of families combined together in unity. Don't forget, you were not always where you are today, and it took for someone else to help you get there. Whether you answered when ***God*** called or not, it wasn't on your own. We are not doing the job that ***God*** expects us to do to bring the lost to Him to be saved. Where is the Love? Where is the Holy Spirit? We make all kinds of excuses for why we can't go certain places or be around certain people. We ought not to make it as though we are better than the next, because **we all fall** short of our blessings. We are not **to judge** others because that **is not our job** or our place. We can only judge their actions and not the person. If we see a drunk, a drug addict, a thief, a liar, a prostitute, or any other characteristics of a human being that is not of ***God***, then we should be doing whatever we can to help that person get better. Don't keep putting them down by laughing and passing judgment on them. What makes you feel you are any better than them? Is it because you're not on the streets and you don't smoke, drink or steal? That doesn't make you better than them. You are in a blessed status right now, but they are an example of what can happen to you if you don't stay in line with ***God's*** Will, so ***thank God*** and watch your judgment on other people. Be proud that **we have a merciful God**. That person was not born that way; there was something that happened in their life along the way that caused them to take that route to put them in that condition. One key factor to always remember is to "***stop***" saying what you wouldn't do, or that can never be me, because you never know how you will end up, especially when you're not walking with ***Christ***. Some of these people may have said the same thing feeling that they were strong enough, until they were put in a situation and were tested. If you continue to say such things and think that you are strong enough to handle certain situations, "you better watch out," because ***Satan*** hears everything you say, and he will put ***your*** "***Faith***" to the test. This is spoken in the Scripture of **Matthew 4:1-11** when he tempted even ***Jesus***. The ***test*** is part of the process where you truly find out just how strong and prepared you really are. Just know that **God** puts us in people's **lives** for more reason than what we choose to believe or see. Within everyone we come in contact with, whether for a moment, a while, or a lifetime, there is always ***God's*** work for us to do somehow or someway. We need to start asking ***God*** to reveal His purpose for what He wants us to do with that person. We may be used to just strengthen that person, help them turn their life around, or just give them the love and support they don't receive from home. It could be from our testimonies, or our downfalls being used as an example of what to do along with who and what to stay away from. We didn't become **Saints** overnight and we still **work** on it **every day**. It could be a ***test*** to see just how ***faithful*** we are, or it could be your last chance to redeem yourself, or it could be that individual's only opportunity to get it right. Would you want to miss that opportunity? We should just be thankful that we have found our way to the light to and be an example to others of how to get there, and watch ourselves to make sure that we don't overstep our boundaries and wind up being in their place. If you want to be a leader, **lead with Christ**. We are not here to stay around "***Saints***" only. Once the lost are in the ***Spirit***, we are to keep it moving and keep reaching out further to touch more ***lost souls***, but keep checking to make sure the "founded" remains in ***Christ***. ***Jesus*** didn't come to save the ***Saints***, He came to save the sick and lost souls, and if we claim to be followers of ***Christ***, then shouldn't we be doing the same things? He came to speak to His saints and give them positions to help **spread the good news** of how to gain ***eternal life***. He didn't just stay in one place and spread the good news, but He walked from city to city as long as He possibly could, while forgiving and saving along the way. How can we **be more like Christ** but limit ourselves from what we do? If the ***Father*** is in ***Jesus***, and ***Jesus*** is in us, what can't we do? One of my favorite scriptures, **Philippians 4:13**, tells us that we can do "***all***" things through **Christ** who **gives** us **strength**. If ***Jesus*** can do it, so can we, but we have to **have** the same "**faith**" as ***Jesus*** did. ***Jesus*** didn't need proof from His Father. ***He knew*** He had the proof within Him and that's why He was able to speak it, touch it, and it was done. He was able to cure diseases, revive the dead, restore health, give sight back, and even drive out demons. You can find some of these miracles in **Matthew 8:23-26, 30 and 9:4-6**.

There are many humans in the world today that can do these things, but it's only by the ***Grace*** of ***God*** and through their **faith** and dedication of their service for the Lord. Some of them don't recognize or realize it because they ***believe*** it is the work of their own hands, but it is **God** who **makes** these **miracles happen**. Be as it may, ***God*** is looking out more for the one coming to be healed, because it's either one or both who holds the ***faith*** in the act that brings that miracle to life. Everyone can't do that today, because we have too much doubt and don't know the ***true*** meaning of "***faith***." We do what we want to do and that is the biggest problem today and why we stay so unhappy. We are being asked to step up and be more honest and serious about our work as ***Servants*** and ***Servant Leaders***. If you are a **"true" child of God**, you will show Him that you are about His business. Are you sure you are a true child of ***God***?

God created us all how He wanted us to be, which was for His intentions of our purpose in this life. He created us with our own looks, our own talents, our own dreams, and our own desires, but we all have the same ***needs***, which

He promised to supply. We all have looks, dreams, talents and desires that are similar, but not the same, because there is always something that makes it different. For our looks; we may look alike, but our DNA differentiates which child we are, the same talents with different aspects, and the same dreams and desires, but with different purposes. When **God** created us, He **created us** in His image, **just like Jesus**. You can find this proof in **Genesis 1:20-27.** We are of ***God***, and ***God*** is of man, woman, child and infant. He created us to be like Him so that we could live like Him, in a Mansion, not a shack, a box, nor a house, but a mansion that is prepared for us. It is a place where there will be no more tears, no sadness, no pain, no hurt, no stealing, no killing, nor any hatred. There will be total and complete happiness, full of laughter, ***Peace*** and joy filled with lots of ***Love***. You can't have ***Peace*** without ***Love***. **God is Love**, who gives all ***Peace***. **Please** stop taking life for granted. We don't have to do anything but love and **let Christ lead the way**. We all need each other in some form or matter. But as written in **Revelation 21:27**, if you are impure and your name do not appear to be written in the Lamb's (Jesus) book of life, you will not see this mansion.

Chapter 3:
God Is Your True Father

I want to shed some light on how the world sees and treats **God**. Keep in mind, this may not apply to everyone, but this is something **we** can all share with ***God's children***. You see yourself right now as just a donated sperm cell and ***God*** was the donor. You know the woman you were birthed to, but you don't know your "real" ***Father***. You don't know that ***God*** is your biological father by nature, but you see your earthly father for some of us; however you know you have a ***Heavenly Father*** out there you've never seen, never met, and only hear about. I'm sure you heard about how "**Great** and **Holy**" He is. How "**Wonderful and Marvelous**" He is. How "**Powerful and Faithful"** He is. How "**Awesome and Mighty**" He is. I'm sure you heard how "**Merciful** and **Spectacular**" He is. How **Good** He is, and that He is a **Healer**, **Provider** and a **Miracle Worker**. You hear all these things about the "**One**" who created you, by word of the mouth from someone else; I'm just curious to know why "***you***" are not curious enough to find out these things for yourself? Why are you not eager to get to know and see Him? Why won't you spend time with Him by yourself and introduce Him to all your family and friends? I'm positively sure that once you introduce Him to them and they see how excited and happy you are, that they are going to want to check Him out for themselves and spend time with Him by themselves. In turn, they will introduce Him to their friends and so forth. Oh how quickly the ***Word*** would spread. You will get excited about Him, but just know and prepare yourself for His **enemy (Satan)**, who **hates** to see **us** smiling and happy and will do just about anything to bring us down; "**if**" we let him. You need to know that he will be right there in your mind putting doubt and trying to show us things and reasons of why we shouldn't believe or **trust God**. ***Satan*** **will reveal his evilness** to us and show us all the things going wrong in our lives and the death of family members just to "**try**" and get us to blame and hate **God**. Remember that Satan doesn't "make" us do anything; he can only tempt us and try to convince us of a good reason to do wrong. The choice is totally up to you to either go right and do what is good, or go left and do what is wrong. **God doesn't "hate" us**. He hates the "things" that the flesh does.

People misconstrue ***God's*** hate to believe that He hates people, but the truth about it is in **Proverbs 6:16**. It tells of the six "***things***" ***God*** hates. He hates ***haughty eyes***, a ***lying tongue***, ***hands*** that shed blood, a ***heart*** with wicked schemes,***feet*** that do evil, ***the damage*** from a false witness, and the "man's" evil mind (***Satan***, His enemy who will "never" bow down). **God loves us**. He is our Rock, our Foundation and our Best Friend. He will be there when everyone else walks away from us. We need to **remember** that **God** didn't promise us that every day would be beautiful, or that we would have eternal life here on earth, so we are going to have bad days and lose those we love one day, unannounced to us. That's why it is so important for us to ***have faith*** and love one another as ***Jesus*** proclaimed before His death. We should **never take anyone for granted**. Remember that everyone has there own characteristics and ways that are none like your own. So we can't expect everyone to think like us, act like us, be like us, or live like us. We all have a gift of our own that is used to help each other come together as one body of Christ. That's why we ***need*** to be there for each other to show others how strong we are and how we got that way.

Have you ever looked at the view behind the eyes of the ***Holy Spirit*** in you? ***God*** doesn't give you more than you can bear, and **He equips you** with everything you need. If you **have total faith** that **God is with you** all the time as long as you are in ***Christ***, has it ever dawned on you that **God places you** right where you need to be for others? That is a test of dedication of your service. Everything is not always about "***you.***" When you help someone else out there is a blessing coming right back to you. ***Blessings*** are not always in the form of money. Most of your blessings come through people and that's why we miss the blessings because we turn our backs too often. There is nowhere in this world that you cannot go or be when you are filled with the ***Holy Spirit*** and ***God's armor*** is around you. The light in you will shine for miles ahead. ***God*** will always protect you as long as you are under His wing, but if you go lurking in a danger field out from underneath His wings, then you can't always expect ***God*** to help you because ***God*** is not in the mist of evilness. ***God*** will be there waiting for you to call on Him so He can snatch you up out of the danger, but if the evilness gets the best of you and you keep going, ***God*** will let you go to give you your space to grow and be strengthened from your mistakes. The most important detail to learn from this is to always know that these situations come about in your life to test your "**faith**." ***God*** wants to know that you still feel the same about Him when things really get rough, and that you trust Him to take care of you. He wants to know that while you are in that storm and He sends someone to you, will you still show them love and support and look out for them, or will you consume yourself with your own problems? You get back from life what you put into it, and if you don't look out for others and help someone else, who is going to help you? Treat the world the way you want the world to treat you. When you have hatred in your heart that is what you will get back in return. You are the only one holding the key to your future and your happiness. You have full access to it; all you have to do is use the key to open the door to all of your dreams, hopes, and desires, but most importantly your ***needs***. You will only know which one is the right door by knowing ***God*** and being led in the right ***Spirit***. ***God*** will never lead you astray, nor will He ever leave you. When you let Satan pull you off the tracks and don't look for ***God's*** help, He will stand by and wait for you to call on Him to rescue you. He is already there, but if you don't call on Him, then you let Him know that you have everything under control and you don't need Him. He will let you go to be on your own because He gives you a ***choice***. He doesn't make you do anything you don't want to do. But the good news is that He's always right there when you are ready and you call. Make sure that you are in ***the right Spirit*** **w**hen you call on Him. The truth of the matter is that you are a ***Child of God***, but until you fully accept the fact that "**GOD IS Your Father**," your mother, your sister and brother; ***God*** is your doctor, your healer, your lawyer, your provider and is in "total and complete" ***control***, then and only then will you truly accept the fact that you are a ***true*** child of ***God.*** We can rest on **God's time** and time is winding down.

Chapter 4:
Love Is The Key

I wanted to know what living a ***Christian life*** was all about, so I had to start living the things I knew and what I was told. If I wanted to make a difference in my life and others, I had to give "***all***" of my problems to ***God*** and let Him work it out. I knew that it would be hard work and require a lot of effort, but I was willing because **God is able**. If I wanted to help other people and be more like ***Christ***, I had to have a relationship with Him and start loving like Christ. **Christ loves "all"** of His children with no exceptions. He may not be pleased with the way things have turned out, but **His love is unconditional**. I couldn't get that confused with the fact that just because we are all His creations, **we** all **have failed** His **purpose** for us and therefore, "***all***" of us are not His children until we fully **accept Him into our hearts**. With this in mind I knew I had to prepare myself to deal with some very mean and nasty folk, but keeping in mind that ***Satan*** is only using that person to try to take me out of my "***Christian***" character. **Satan** only **tries** to show us that it's impossible to excuse someone for his or her behavior and still have ***love*** for that person. That's not a hard task to do because we prove that "fact" every time someone we want to hold on to mistreat us, cheats on us, beat on us, steal from us, lie to us, and walk away from us. No matter what that person does, we are destined to keep that person around for as long as we can, and we just can't find it in our hearts to walk away or make them leave. We still **find a way to love** them and sometimes even more than before. That is a ***choice*** of how we choose to behave toward one another. ***Satan can't*** make us do anything we don't want to do. We were created with ***love*** in our ***hearts*** and if you have ***God*** in your ***heart***, your ***love*** will shine like never before, and you can be at ***peace*** with any situation. In order to be able to ***love*** someone else, you must first love yourself, but without conceit. You must **love yourself** so that you will know what **love** feels like to **receive it**; that way it will make ***love*** that much easier to give away. The most important aspect is to first know what love is. **Love is** absolute, beautiful, caring, a commitment, dedicated, delightful, devotional, effective, empathetic, emotional, encouraging, faithful, forgiving, giving, grateful, hopeful, intellectual, joyful, kind, loving, loyal, magnificent, needful, outstanding, passionate, patient, pleasant, pleasing, powerful, reliable, respectful, responsible, satisfying, sweet, thankful, touching, true, unconditional, understanding, unique, unstoppable, victorious, withstanding, wonderful, worthy, yearning, and zealous. You should always make your love true because **God is** Love and **the Truth**, and so shall be ***your love***. You can't have one without the other. If you don't have ***God***; you don't have ***Love***. Without ***God*** your love is not true. Let's learn to **love "in spite of"** and not because of**.** **God** is ***Christ***, and Christ is in us and there is nothing we can't do. If **God still loves** us in spite of, then we should love each other the same way.

Just **think about** it, if you fill your life with **love**, you can conquer and achieve ***a life of abundance***, which is already promised to us. If you love yourself and the things you do, as well as others around you and the things about them while focusing your attention on love, there is no room for deceit, envy, hatred, or jealousy, which is all despised by ***God***. It's hard for me to understand why we make it so hard to achieve the good life we all seek. We would rather do something to make things hard and difficult for ourselves rather than focus on the things that make us feel good. We are so busy trying to please others that we don't even focus on what "we" want and the things that we know that makes us happy. We **imitate** others to fit in instead of being ourselves. Whatever one does in the world, we are right there to do the same, regardless of how people deem it to be something negative. We will always find **something** out of it to be **positive** just so it can fit our standards. How can we be ourselves if we can't even accept the things about ourselves as far as what we like and what we do? We will change our whole appearance just to fit in and feel appreciated or accepted by society. Some of us need to step outside of ourselves and sit back and watch the way we act from the things we do and say, and then ask ourselves "what do we really want to do and be?" We are so stuck on ourselves that we ignore the options for a good life by feeling that we can make our own lives the way we want it to be and expect it to be a good one. We all have our own ways and need to make a change for the better, but not just for ourselves. I believe a lot of people would change without hesitation if we really seek change. The truth being told is that we need to make a change for Christ's sake to show Him that "***We***

are" worthy of His cause for coming to save us. His death was about ***Love***, and that's what we need to start showing more of. The world we ought to want to fit in is the one that ***God*** has promised us. There is no better life to live. Everything we do, the first thing we should ask ourselves is, "**What would Jesus do**?" After all, He is the ***real*** reason you are still here right now at this present moment to hear the truth about our expectations as children of ***Christ***. He has the power to take your life at any given moment, but because of His unconditional love for us, He gives us the option to live out our purpose if we desire it. He has a purpose for you and that's why you are still here. There is no more time for play; this world is slowly but surely going to "***Hell***." Let's all **stand for CHRIST** before we all **fall in Hell.** If **God** loves us with all of our hang ups and mistakes and **still blesses us** and gives us chance after chance to get it right; don't you think it's about time you start loving Him back? If you are ready to love Him; start by **trusting Him**, **believing** in **Him** and most importantly; **have "Faith"** in Him. If you feel you already love Him you should already know where I'm going with this. If you have ***faith*** in Him you already ***trust*** and ***believe***. If you believe in ***God***, you should be smart enough to know that He is not a ***God*** of lies. As it is written in the book of **Revelation 22:18-20**, "***nothing***" is to be added to the Bible; for to whoever does, plague will be added to them, and whoever "***removes***" words from the ***Bible***, it will be taken away from their share of the tree of life. If you believe in ***God***, you know there is nothing in between ***Heaven*** and ***Hell***. So you either believe or you don't. If He says come to me and **ask** and **it is given**, then you should be following ***Jesus*** because He is going to walk you right into all of your ***blessings*** of a life of abundance and **peaceful eternity** that's already prepared and waiting for you. That is your beginning and your end. But in order to get there you must first be in the right ***Spirit***. As it is written in the ***Bible*** in **Romans 8:29;** "He who searches our **hearts** knows the mind of the Spirit because the **Spirit intercedes for the saints** in accordance with ***God's*** will." **God's will** is for us to **be** just **like Christ** so we can live a good life here on earth and an even better one at the end of our journey. What do you think your journey is about? **He is** standing **there** watching and waiting, **with open arms**, for you to **come to Him** so He can make it "all" better for you. Most of us can't get away from our problems or the issues in our lives because we run to the Man of the world instead of ***God***. If you **want** "**life,**" start **walk**ing **with Christ**, and if **you want "death**," then keep **walk**ing **with Satan**. In order to really have true love and live a meaningful life, you must **know God**. ***Have Faith*** in **God**. He **is** the way to **your salvation**.

Chapter 5:
Why We Should Stand For Christ

Why don't we stand up enough for **Christ**? Anywhere they tell us we can't include ***our beliefs*** in what we do as far as in our work place, in the schools, and now they're trying within the prisons, that ought to concern all of us. That should tell us something about the word "Christ." Why and what is it that they don't want us to know or tell each other? Why is ***Christ*** such a big problem in the world? Some **choose** to **believe** that **Jesus** was not sent, nor was He **the Messiah**. Some choose to believe that ***Mary*** was sent, and some choose to believe there is only ***God***. I don't understand how one could believe such things. If you read the Bible, and you **believe in God**, why do you **choose** not to believe **His Word**? If **Jesus is** nobody, why can't we talk about **Christ** wherever we go? If He is nobody, what can one stand to lose if we talk about Him? They don't want to hear how ***marvelous*** and ***wonderful*** He is. There is a reason we can't **talk about Christ**, and that's because they don't want us to know the ***Truth***; "***Jesus.***" Is He not the one who wakes us up every morning and helps us to get from A to Z safely? Is He not the one who cares for our children and our loved ones keeping them safe and out of harms way when they're not with us? If you believe that **Jesus is** Christ, **Christ is in you**, and that **Christ is a spirit**, then where did the spirit of Christ come from? It comes from ***God***. ***God*** has to send the spirit somehow, don't you think? Furthermore, if you truly and wholeheartedly ***love***, trust and believe ***God*** the ***Father*** why would you doubt His Word? Do you really and honestly think that ***God*** would have us to believe something not true about Him? This ***Bible*** has been around for centuries, with the same readings of the gospel. Would He have not destroyed this book like He has caused destruction to things in the world before ours? What would be the gain for ***God***? He already has everything He needs. He created us; we didn't create Him. **Don't** let anyone **take** your belief away from you. Don't let anyone else come and persuade you to believe anything other than what you know in your heart. That is where **God is**, in **your Heart**, which He keeps beating for you. **Jesus** is your **bread to life** and the **Spirit** is your **water** to quench your thirst; and **you "need" all** three **to survive** this cruel and evil world. You can find this truth written in **John 6:32-35**. You go and **seek the truth** and **God** will reveal it to you if you truly want to know. Remember that He knows your heart and every thought. There's nothing you can hide from Him because He will bring **"**everything**"** in your life to the light. You can ***verify*** that in **Luke 8:17.** Stand for Christ, and if someone has a problem with what you are doing, then you **activate your faith** and tell them "**it's in God's hands** and if you have a problem with it, take it up with Him."

What I have to say may not apply to everyone, but if it does, then you shouldn't be offended; you should take it as constructive criticism. Now that your eyes and ears are attentive, open your heart and receive it so you can apply it to your life and make a change for the good not just for yourself, but for others around you as well. You must start from the inside and work your way outside to make the change. I want you all to know that whatever I speak about; go both ways for me and for you. This is insight I have just leaned about and **chose to** make a **change**, and the rest of what I'm listening to now is what I'm "going" to change. I will represent a "***Christ-like***" life, striving hard every day to get there. I am not claiming to be perfect or holier than thou, but I am serious about my Father's business. We all take part in the things that put us in the positions that cause us so much pain and grief in the end. We all know that in life you get back what you put out, and there is no if, ands, or buts about it. One question I have is why do we stay so mad and angry at people to where we start to **hate** when we know that's not a characteristic of ***Christ***? **Hate** is a characteristic of **Satan**. This is a trait we can all **live without**. **Satan** represents enough of that. We have accepted ***Satan*** in our hearts the moment we start hating each other. That is when we show him that we will do anything for him. You are now his puppet on a string. **Satan tempts** us to perform all kinds of evil acts that cause us to believe that we are getting something out of the deal and we believe it is ok. He tells us to **steal;** so we take things that do not belong to us. He tells us to **cheat**; we believe no one can see us. He tells us to **lie;** we believe we are so good at it and no one will know. He tells us to **kill**; they don't deserve to be here anyway. He tells us to **disobey our parents;** they don't know what they're talking about, and they just don't want us to have fun; and some believe they are even jealous. He tells us to **hate** your God, and we believe that He doesn't help us or love us because our life is a wreck; so where is He? He tells you to put the **blame** on **someone else**; let him or her work their way out of it. We do all of these evil acts without ever once taken in consideration someone else's feelings. Maybe the person you are taking advantage of may not see the act, but **God sees and hears it all**, and that is where your concern should come in. There is nothing to be proud of in these acts. You are taking away someone's peace, joy, and happiness. Somewhere along the lines yours will be taken away too. Why are we so content with doing what ***Satan*** wants us to do? Why are we so caught up in pleasing man? Man doesn't give a hoot about who we are or what we do as long as it doesn't get in the way of his affairs. Man will do anything to keep us down and make sure we stay down. Man will use us both mentally and physically. Man makes us cry, sad, depressed, and it's all because he makes sure that we don't make it in this world that he thinks is his. **Thank God** we have a merciful ***God*** who is in control of it all.

The problem is that **we are** still **"stuck" in the World**. We are so adapted to **Satan's ways** that it's hard to make a change for something good. We think more of ourselves and make our lives about "***me***," that we don't take time to help someone else. We are looking for a hand out instead of putting a hand in. This is an act of **selfishness**, which **God** also **despises**. This has ***Satan*** written all over it; all of these are his characteristics. **Satan** has you to **perform** all of these **acts** because he knows **that** they will **keep you out** of the Kingdom **of Heaven**. He doesn't tell you that when he whispers these things in your ear and play with your mind that it is just a test to make sure you still trust, believe, and love your ***God***. **Satan** was also a **child of God**, so he **knows the Bible** inside and out, but he fell in his own trap of deception and was **kicked out of Heaven** to be on his own. On his own he felt that he could take the world and make it his, and ever since then he has been trying and for the most part he's been succeeding. We always use the same excuse about what this person done to me, how they made me feel, or how we don't like how they act. We need to stop and ask ourselves, "does ***God*** see any of these characteristics in me, and would I want Him to feel that way about me?" **God** can change circumstances, yes, and so can we because He has fully **equipped us with** enough **knowledge**, **wisdom**, and **strength** to do so.

We put ourselves in everything we go through that tears us apart and make us miserable, and that's simply because we don't **know God** enough to **trust Him** to work it out for us. There is no reason to be mad, upset, disappointed, or discouraged. We "all" make mistakes and have poor or bad judgment at times. Like Martin said; "***no one*** is immune to the trials and tribulations of ***life***," but just remember that it **is a test**. Don't let that get you down, because you can turn every situation around simply by making ***wiser*** choices and decisions. That means to **let God guide you**. It just takes time. Before doing something, ask yourself some valuable questions about what you're about to do and how it will affect you long term. The amount of time it takes depends on the length of time it takes for you to straighten your life out and **get** it **right with God**. We have to start thinking for ourselves and not blame others for the reason why things aren't going right for us. **We are** all **responsible** for our own actions and the outcome of our own lives. We can point people in the right direction with the knowledge given to us, but we can't make them follow. We can not put them in Heaven or Hell.

We can have the life we want, but we choose otherwise. We follow Satan and we wonder why we continuously fail. We are the ***cause*** of the ***effect*** of our own life. **Everything we say** and do is what **we** are **claim**ing for our lives. The way we treat others is how we get treated. ***God*** wants to know how many people really stand for Him. We need to stop complaining so much. We want everything to be right for us and suit our situations. Everything doesn't work for everybody. Some people may like things this way and others may like it that way. How do you satisfy everyone? You can't; it's impossible to please a bunch of ***ungrateful people***. They want everything to be how they want it to be regardless if it is beneficial to them or not, and they usually don't realize it until the end result. ***God*** wants things to go His way too; the difference is **He promises** you **peace**, **joy, love**, **happiness**, **abundance**, and **eternal life** at the end of your journey. Eternal life is everlasting. **God gives** all that and more; what do you give? What can you promise and live up to? Refusing to do things ***God's way*** only makes "your" life harder. Try it His way and see if you like it. What can you lose? **Remember**, what you put out is what you get in return, there's **no doubt** about it. Just think about it; anyone with a heart full of love is surrounded by people who love them.

People who have hatred in their hearts are surrounded by hateful people. Life works hand in hand.

Chapter 6:
How to Fight off Evil

I **love all** five of my **children** dearly, but I know that they all have their own personalities and their own ways, so I expect them to be different. They are not going to say and do the same things as each other. The one thing I will never do is give up on them no matter what. I will do everything in my power to guide them in the right direction, but it is up to them when they get out on their own to continue to live the life they have been taught. I will not take responsibility for their actions when I know I have taught them how to make Christian decisions that will make a good impression for their future. I will stand behind them 100% when they are right, but when they are wrong they are left to figure out how to make it right. I still refuse to give them up to Satan without a fight. I have learned that when I say things like "I can't take it, they don't listen, or they are old enough and it's time for them to be out there on their own to **learn** from their own **mistakes**," Satan is all up in it and hears everything I say and will now use everything I just said against me. Even though it may be time for them to go and experience life on their own, I wouldn't let them go without attempting to keep helping them regardless of their issues, because **Satan** will take and use them to his advantage to do his **dirty** work while keeping them in sin. Parents let's not give them up without a fight. If I continue to do my job as a mother and protector, keep them prayed up, love them, and accept what I know and believe; that they have their own personality and ways, they will be **in God's hands** which is **the safest place** in the universe. He will be right there to protect them. I can safely let them go. Think about the things and time it took for you to become a better person. You didn't change overnight and neither will they. We as **parents** can help more than we care to, but that means getting and **stay**ing **involved** in their life. We can't afford to give them privacy now-a-days. We have to make sure everything is good with them at home as well as in school. Parents take control over your children and claim your position while disregarding their attitude to be upset. Sit down and talk to them. Teach them the real and true values of life so they can start to make a change that will eventually make a difference. Stop making excuses for what you can't do and live for what you can do. Our children don't have to be the way they are today if we instill the "same values." We can only do that when more adults decide to come together as one about the same concerns and issues and continue to teach our children "together" about what's right and wrong with the things they do and how it affects other people. More importantly, we need to teach them that they will be judged for "everything" they do. This will not become effective until we are fed up and tired of all of this madness around us. We should be at that point by now. So why don't we all come together to do something about it? What kind of role model are you? Treat them the way you want ***God*** to treat you.

None of what I'm about to say excuses children, but just speaking the truth so we can help one another to better **grasp** the concept of **life**. We ask our children to do things. We want them to change their ways and treat people with respect, be honest to each other, **love each other** and basically do what we ask and things will be much better. We get along better; now doesn't it make life a little easier and simpler? We reward them from time to time for doing something good to let them know we appreciate them. Well, ***God*** requires the same from us. So every time you form your lips to say anything to anyone about how they are not doing something right or how they don't listen and need to change their ways; stop and ask yourself, have I done any of these things ***God***, "my ***Father***" has asked me to do? If we do what we're asked we don't only **set** an **example**, but we can **be** an **example**. We want nothing but the best of the best for the ones we ***love***, and that is what ***God*** wants for us. **We are** created in the image of **Him**. That's in **Genesis 1:27.** So whatever He is capable of doing so are we because we are equipped with the abilities to do it. **Philippians 4:13**, one of ***my favorite scriptures*** says, "We can do all things through ***Christ*** who strengthens us." We give advice and tell people to learn from our experiences and look at how we're struggling when we don't have to, and we push so much because we want them to live a life of abundance. Well, ***God*** has sent **His Son** to be **an example** of how if we just love and share the knowledge about Him and His expectations of us, which is the promise He has made for us; we can have eternal life from our ***faith*** and ***obedience***. Everything we have been told tells us about a reward that would make us happy if we **choose to live for Christ.**

This is found in **Romans 6:23. God** doesn't **require** for **us to** do any labor, all He asks is that we **love**. "**Love conquers all**."

For **children**, anytime **you are** being taught something right, you get an attitude and start throwing out **spiteful** words such as, "my parents don't know what's best for me, they don't really love me, my parents are trying to stop me from having fun, and my parents want to see me fail." Once you feel you're on a roll and you get just one of your friends to agree, you start throwing out mean and nasty things such as, "I hope they get hit by a car, a bus, or a train, I hope they die, they make me sick, I wish they weren't my parents, or I wish they would go away and get out of my life." These are phrases that go way back in history that most of us have hoped or wished for about our parents, but **thank God** that He **is** a **merciful God** and knows our hearts, and our wishes never came true, for some of us, at the time we were speaking them because later on this passes over and you are glad at another moment that they are still around. It is wise to watch the words you speak**,** because in essence, you are asking for these things to be done. Children, you can learn from the past of your parents. Everything we tell you are things that we have either been through, seen others go through, or still live through today. You are warned of these things because we don't want you to go through the same things we've been through. It's hard enough going through life's challenges and experiences on our own, but it's even worst to watch your child go through them. We inform you about the challenges and experiences you will face to give you heads up. We ask you to look at our lives so you can see the end results of some of the things we put ourselves through by not thinking first, observing, or **remember**ing what **we** already **know.** How can you learn something from someone who has never been through anything? You will go through trying times to make you stronger and knowledgeable, but they don't have to last a long time. The best teacher is someone who has been through a lot. This person would be used as a testimony for survival, especially if they are in ***Christ***. Some parents seem to care so much about their own lives that they will get their children just about anything just to make them happy or keep them out of their faces regardless of how much **damag**ing it can be to **their future**. I don't knock anyone for what they do to make a living, but some of these things are what makes the children today do all sorts of evil things. The clothesline that shows your butt and breast gives off a negative vibe about some of these females. I'm not putting anyone out there, but these outfits are the cause of females being called out of their names and treated like female street workers. The biggest motto, "shake what your momma gave you," and "flaunt it if you got it," is a way to show females how to get a guy but not keep one. Some of the styles are cute just by the design, but it expresses a statement that is not positive. These outfits can send off mixed signals and cause problems for females. Why do we create designs that speak about sex? Why is it that sex is used to sell? What happened to using your heart and your intelligence to get what you want? Whatever it is you use to get what you want, when you lose what you used, you also lose what you gained. The sad part about it is that society is so caught up in it just being a style that they don't realize the reason of why males treat females the way they do. Everything has to perfectly advertise in order to sale and it has to sound good, but what is the end result? I would like for every female to truly listen to the rap music lyrics that are out there. The videos and the words used in the song speak the truth about all the corruption in this world today. Females are dancing and shaking to the very same lyrics that are speaking about a female dog, a tramp, how easy it is to get a female, and all the nasty things she will do to anyone just to a make a quick buck. Some of these females are so happy just to be in a video letting these guys rub all over them, having them sexing each other one after another, and everybody is on everybody. What is that all about? There is a better way to represent yourself and what you stand for. This is just another way to sale their music. I am not criticizing anyone's style for music; I am just trying to shed some light on how we females make choices without thinking about the consequences. I know there are some females out here that claim they don't care, but I know that is so far from the truth. We have little girls out here watching us to help them make a decision on what they want to be when they grow up. In your eyes you may feel that they have their own life to live and they don't have to be like you, but in reality, they look up to us and it is our responsibility to be a good role model for them. ***God*** didn't give us what we have to abuse it. We have it so we can use it for positive motivation. Our life is not just about ourselves. ***Everything*** we do makes a difference to someone else.

The f**emales are** out there s**tripping for money**. Do you really feel that this is all your body is good for? Ladies, the next time you go out to take your clothes off for these guys, just pay attention to some of the things they say and while you are at it try to read the lips of some of the **guys** who are **watch**ing **you.** Better yet, act as though you don't want to go over to him and watch how quickly your name changes. Is it really all worth it in the end? Do you really not have any dignity for yourself? I know you do, because you have more respect for yourself. It is your actions that make it seem as though you don't. It's not about whatever you have to do to pay the bills because there is always a better way. It's the life you **choose** to live that will predict the kind of person you may turn out to be if you don't find **Christ** before it's too late. I'm not knocking your lifestyle, but you can do so much more with your life than entertain these guys with your body. Most of them are married and shouldn't even be in that spot. It is not your fault, but if these spots were not available; where would they be? Don't use the excuse, "if it's not me, then it will be someone else" because **it's not about** someone else, it's about **you** and you **only**. Females, we need to have more class about ourselves. It's not about another female being jealous when they're trying to **give** you **good advice;** that is someone sent to help you. We are here to **contribute** to society for **something good**. I guarantee you that the men who are married talk about these same females to their wives informing them of why they would never mess with those kinds of females. Most men, real men anyway, want a sexy and respectable classy lady to stand by them. I know there is at least one female, who will be the first to make an excuse for why they do it, and the main reason would be for money, but money is not everything. Believe it or not there is more to life than just money. It is how we make the money that makes the difference. As stated in **I Timothy 6:10**, the **love of money** is the root of all **evil;** and this world is all about ***greed***. Isn't this the reason why **God destroyed the world** the first time? Everyone was out of control with marriage and their wicked ways, and now He has to watch the same thing all over again. How sad is that? His heart is filled with ***grief***. This fact is written in **Genesis 6:6-7. God created** one **man** for every one woman to live a happy and prosperous life in unity. It's hard to tell that because the men are killing each other, others are locked away, and the boys in blue are killing the rest. Most people will never know the truth because we are always looking for more than what we have. They don't know how to make a relationship last or **make a marriage work** because they are lacking ***Christ***. Greed is becoming a very big part of the wickedness of the world today**.** We all have to do a lot more **grow**ing **in Christ**. If you are not sure of yourself, then you need to seek more of ***Christ*** for direction. **Put God first** and He will give you what you need.

Chapter 7
How Did We Get There?

There are so many questions about how we all got to where we are now starting from the children up to the adults. There are some questions we should ask, and some things we should think about. We don't trust and love each other enough. We don't appreciate each other's worth. Why is it that we always want someone to **notice** the outside before they get to know **the inside?** We wonder why others can't **see the good** person **inside** of us, and they mistreat us and walk away. Men do not make things any easier for women. Men are about to be extinct if they don't get their acts together. All this evil they do out here in the world; killing, robbing, and beating on women. There is **no excuse** for it, but it happens. When will it ever **stop**? They run from place to place to see how many females they can have chasing and fighting over them just to give conversation with the rest of the guys. Women, how and **why** do we **deal with it** and constantly put up with it without wanting to make a change? We deserve so much more out of life from a man, but we have to first love ourselves. ***Most*** men play the hard role like they don't have any compassion in them. They are so bitter and cold and don't know how to be responsible. Most men won't show a woman his true feelings. Some blame it on their parents, but we are all responsible for the way our lives turn out once we become young adults. Men you have experienced the way things were growing up, so you have the opportunity to **make it better** when you get out on your own, but **you choose** to continue down **the** same **path**. You speak about your father not being around and never being there for you; shouldn't that make you want to be a better man? You should want to teach your son or other boys and young men the things you missed out on. Don't use the excuse that you don't know because you were never taught. **You know** what you wanted and what you missed out on.

Women need to be closer to our children to help make our sons to become gentlemen and our daughters to become respectable young ladies. We need to be examples of how our daughters should welcome a "real" man into her life. We need to be there to support her as well as be a friend that she can talk to about her problems so she doesn't take them to someone else. We need to teach our sons how to be real men so they will know how they should treat women. Let them know they should treat a woman the same way they would want a man to treat his mother. Husbands and wives; why do you let others come into your bedroom and join in with what you **believe God** brought together? ***God*** only brings two people together, one man and one woman to produce a family of their own. ***God*** didn't make man for man and woman for woman. That is wrong and the truth needs to be told, regardless if know one wants to hear or not. No one should be offended because the truth is the truth and a fact is a fact. You are destroying your destiny by altering **God's time** and effort He took to create you. Do you care if you are hurting ***God*?** That should make all the difference in the world to you. That way of lifestyle is very displeasing to ***God***. It's time to stop intervening in ***God***'s purpose for His creations. That is not a part of what ***God*** would do, but it is what ***Satan*** would do. This is **God's world** in which He created you as the perfect being just the way He wanted you so that you would be able to live out your purpose here on earth. Can you see or feel the pain you are causing to your Father? Do you truly not care? It seems like the more ***God*** tries to give us a better life; the more we cause destruction and ruin it. Does ***God*** mean "anything" to you at all? I would never make it as though I was never out there doing the things I wasn't supposed to, or make it like I'm better than or holier than the rest, but it was never the way they do it today. I have attempted to do some things that were not **pleas**ing to **God** which caused me to see the destruction we are headed for, and that made me want to change my whole lifestyle. Our home is our private space, and that's where most of these things should be kept as long as it is within the line of ***Christ***. Most of my doing was out with my ex-husband, but that still shouldn't have given me reason to do it. **I was lost** back then; now I am walking with ***Christ*** where I plan to stay until He returns. That was the best decision I ever made.

The video games that teach skills of how to kill, rob, and destroy are more distractions created to keep our children in sin. I don't buy these games for my son because I don't condone the violence in them, but I use the word "we" because I don't want anyone to feel that I am picking. These are the games that we will hurt and kill each other over just so our children can be the first to have them; and we wonder why our children are filled with so much hatred and don't have any respect for their elders today. The things we buy our children make us responsible for their behavior. We are in control over their lives, because we are the providers and their protectors. There are so many educational games out there, but it seems like parents are more exited about their children having games that are violent. Stop promoting violence in your children's life and start promoting education and career moves for their future. If you want your child to be about something, you should get them games to help advance their skills for education. Choose the games that give them options on how to become educated and successful in life. They also have games of sports, which can help them with a career move after school. Some of these games promote sex, drugs, and money which are a big contribution to society that is destroying more than half the population, because the children are becoming masters of it. We are not responsible for what our children do when they are out there on their own, but it will make a huge difference if we teach them the right way while they are young.

Drugs are not only used to make money, but also to seduce and lure women into a bedroom. You can't trust anyone to fix you a drink or have someone to watch it for you when you are out. You can barely trust them in your own home for fear of them putting something in it. It's much safer to have them to get you a can or bottle that hasn't been opened. A lot of people want to do drugs under the impression that they won't get hooked. ***Drugs*** are laced with so many chemicals that people are literally dying just to get a high. They see the end result of a friend or loved one, but **Satan convinces** them that it is safe and that they can handle it. These drugs can cause people to sell their bodies, perform sexual favors, attempt to commit suicide, and even steal from their own homes and families just to get them. The "***best***" high in life is ***Christ***. **Money** is something we all like to have. There is nothing wrong with wanting to have money, but it makes a world of difference in your purpose of wanting it and what you choose to do with it. The difference of what makes that money evil is how you use and spend it. When we start making money out to be what we love, it then becomes the root of evilness. Money comes to us so we can save and be in the position to help other people in time of need. That is a blessing for others. **Sex** is a very big issue today, and it is used to manipulate just about everyone in the world. Women know men are crazy about them, so they use their bodies to their advantage to get what they want. Women play a big part in the reason why men cheat on the one they are with. No, women are not responsible for the decision to cheat, but we are in control of the situation and how it plays out. Women know they are enticing men when they make a decision to put on certain clothing. Some wear these outfits because of the style and others wear it to get attention because of their "***insecurities***." I don't care what any woman says about this statement because it is true. I am living proof, and I will speak up and tell the truth when no one else will. I was one who used to wear tight pants because I wasn't built the way other females were with all the big butt and big breast. I felt like I needed to be noticed for something else to make up for what I was lacking, and the only thing I felt I had going for myself was the way I walk. I did it because I wanted to be "***noticed***." I didn't have since enough back then to see and understand that I was doing it just so the guys would pay attention to me. Females are in denial when they claim that the clothing they wear is not for attention, especially when the front of their shirt has a "v" all the way down to the bottom line of their cleavage. That is a turn on for men and we all know it, so why do it when it can cause chaos? Once a guy notices you, all he has to do is compliment you, smile, and whisper something good in your ear and it is over. It's a "game" for men and they love it. They hunt and prey. They stand around each other making bets about which female they are going to have sex with. Most of them win every time. I am not saying “all” men, but majority rules. I am not just picking on the females about sex because everyone is doing it, but I am making a valid point about how women and their bodies are used for products to sell. Society uses females in order to attract the attention of potential customers. Take a look around at the advertisements and they will confirm my statements. You don't see men showing their bodies, but you do see women.

Everyone wants to have sex because "everyone is doing it." It has gotten so bad over the years that even homosexuals are coming out of the closet. This is not being said to discourage, hurt or upset anyone, but right is right and wrong is wrong, and when we stop thinking so much about ourselves we will admit to what is true. I don't knock anyone for what they do, but when it is a problem for what ***God*** has done for us, it becomes personal to me. I am no better than the next woman, but I do want and strive to make my life as "close" to perfect in **God's eyes** as I possibly can. I know that I may not even come close to, but my effort will appear to be that way. I pray that we all will have that same feeling for ***Christ***. We will sin, but some sins we can make a change in our hearts to stop even if it's just for ***Christ*** alone. **God created** Adam and Eve, and as far as I know, that was man and woman. We all make excuses for doing what is against **God's law**, and not enough people will step up and speak the truth about it. In every relationship it should be one man and one woman. We altar everything about **God's creations** because "we" don't like the way He brought things to life. This should bother a lot of people only because it is against our Father's purpose for us. I'm not saying that we shouldn't love them, but we need to do more praying for them to get back with ***God*** where they ought to be. We can't live the standards He has set for us, so we choose to go out here and change them to fit our standards. Without a care in the world about the consequences, we are having sex with just about anybody, and that is very scary. I know and I am prepared for a lot of people to throw punches about me speaking the truth, but "I" see this pain behind ***God's*** eyes because I care. I love "all" of ***God's children*** and I just want us "all" to get it right. I want you to hear it from the Creator Himself. How much more pain does He have to suffer before it will matter to you? This is not how **God intended** for us to live, and because we don't care, we make this life of our own. The truth needs to be told and not sugar coated. It's not ok when we stand to tell **God** that He **made a** mistake in the **way** He created this world. We show Him that when we decide to recreate it to work for ourselves. How can you be that bold? Why don't you care? **God loves you** and He lives for you. Why is it so hard for you to live right for Him? It is so hard to trust anyone now-a-days. No one seems to care about even their own life and where it is headed. We need to stop and **check ourselves**. This world is not just about sex, drugs and money.

These are all characteristics of ***Satan***. A "change" has to start somewhere, so why not start in your home first. It is up to us as people and parents to **take back** what belongs to us. To the parents; we need to take back our rightful place to gain the respect we deserve from our children, because **we are** in control and **responsible** for them reaching their ***God*** given destiny. **God gave** us our children and whether we planned them or were prepared or not, we got them because **God knew** that we were strong enough and equipped to handle the job. As a parent we just don't see or ***believe*** it because our hearts & minds are not focused on the greatest gift we can ever receive in life. Some of us just don't recognize it because we're too busy being **caught up** in our own lives and the things "we" want to do, instead of owning up to the responsibility we helped create by making early decisions. These were decisions we thought we were responsible enough to make when we made the ***choice*** to lie down. That's when you opened yourself up to be tested to see if you were really ready to **be responsible**. We need to make some changes with the music we listen to, how we communicate about sex and drugs with our children, and how we deal with our money. We need to change how we view ourselves. I'm not knocking anyone for the ***choice*** they make in ***life*** because that would **be** judgmental on my part, and I am not **in the position** nor am I the Judge of anyone's mistakes or choices because I'm not perfect myself, and I do not always make wise choices. I am just **speak**ing **the truth** about the **facts** of today's society. Please take notice that I have not ***excluded myself*** in anything I have spoken out about. I am here as **God** has **led** me to be; **to "help"** us see and recognize our mistakes, and to realize that it's not too late to get it right as long as you have breath in your body. But we can only do that with the strength we find in ***God***. Let Him take over your life so you can get the best for yourself. Don't let these addictions become your God. Be a testimony, not a statistic. Replace sex with ***Love***, drugs with ***Christ***, and money with "Faith."

Chapter 8:
Understanding The Truth

People in today's society are so messed up by their attitudes. I would like to point out a true fact that we don't pay attention to which makes a world of difference for what causes so many people to explode. We all have a job to do in this world to make it continue to go around. However, our jobs are supposed to benefit everyone in a positive way, but we just don't realize it. We need to take time from ourselves and show appreciation for the assistance from the ones that we call upon for help. When you call someone, you are expecting that person to help you with whatever situation you are dealing with at that time. In this day and era, it is not that easy to get help. We have people on the job who don't really appreciate or value their positions because they are just out to get a paycheck. These kinds of people are the ones who make it hard for people to get along with each other. If they really don't care about being at work day in and day out, why would they care about helping someone else? We have a lot of people filling positions based on their school education instead of their mentality. Just because someone has the knowledge of a position and completes their education and gets a piece of paper to prove their skills, that doesn't always mean that they are equipped for the position. Some employers select candidates because they have an associate or bachelors degree based on the fact that it sounds "highly intelligent," but the candidates have no people skills or patience. How can they truly be an asset to the company? I thought we open a business to have clientele that will help expand the business to increase the profit. There are so many people who don't care about their business just as long as they can make money. They could care less about losing a few "unsatisfied" customers as long as the business is still going. That kind of attitude works it way down from the top of the chain, and it is one of the biggest reasons that a lot of businesses go under. No one really recognizes it because they can't see the truth. It's kind of hard to keep a business when you slowly but surely lose customers. I mean after all, they are the ones that keep you in business. Just because someone has a degree, that doesn't mean they are "qualified" to "handle" the job. Don't make your business all about money because if you lose your customer's you lose your business.

There are people going to school for nursing degrees that will be watching over our family members. This should be a concern and taken very seriously because it takes more than a piece of paper to attend to the sick and elderly, and **God forbid** they should care for infants and toddlers. The elderly patients deserve love and patience for all of the things they had to endure just to make a living. The infants and toddlers need patience and understanding because they have not been through anything in life. Some of the elderly people can be very difficult to deal with, but they don't mean to be that way. Some of them have been mistreated for so long they just can't take it anymore. We are blessed compared to what they had to go through. You need love, patience, and understanding to deal with these clients. It is not fair that they should have to suffer because you chose a position that "you" knew you were not equipped to handle. We all know the level of our strengths and what we are willing to deal with, but we put money first. That's the price you pay when you make your job about money instead of about helping other people. When you put money first, you welcome all kind of problems and issues into your life little by little, which in turn, causes us to become so miserable, selfish and hateful. When you don't do your nursing job effectively, you cause pain to the client and their families because now they see that someone isn't doing their job right and that can cause emotional problems. That means there may be some unnecessary drama, which in the end can possibly cause someone to explode and fly off the handle.

You have some people who do customer service by phone and they don't have "any" people skills at all. They can't handle clients calling them up with attitudes. There will always be someone who is upset about something that went wrong with their service, and they need someone to assist them with their problem. If you are not patient and understanding, how can you help resolve the issue? You are in a position of customer service. That means to service the customer, not upset the customer. "***Service***" means to help. That also goes for the caller. You are in a position where the associate has all of your information which includes your name, your address, your phone number and most of the time your social security number. You call up an associate who tries to assist you, and just because you feel like giving someone a hard time, you try to make things harder for the person trying to help you. They do the best they can, considering their position they hold within the company. They have to follow certain rules and procedures in order to do their job effectively. When that is not good enough for an individual, they start throwing orders around about what someone is going to do for them, and how the customer service associate is not really helping them; some even have the nerve to tell the associate that they are useless along with all the other mean and nasty things they say to try and make the associate feel worthless on their job. In the meantime, they never take in consideration that, this person has "all" of their information. That is a lot of power to have over someone who has just caused your day to go from good to bad or bad to worst. The only person that would act upon such a situation is one of **Satan's own**. No one ever knows what kind of mood a person is in because we take people's kindness for granted. On either end, both parties know where the other one is. This could cause serious and dangerous actions to be taken out of anger. These are situations that seriously need to be taken into consideration when you are providing or looking for help. In this world today, it would be wise to watch your attitude and the way you treat people. Your actions affect everyone around you in some form, shape, or matter. If your heart isn't in what you chose to do, then you should try something that you love to do and what truly makes you happy. We all have a gift for **do**ing **God's work** in which we are best at, but we have to seek it to find it.

Why don't we understand that we are not the judges over anyone's life? We were not given the position to decide who lives and who dies. **Let God** take care of those who do us wrong. We feel we should make the decision on how someone should be punished. If someone does us wrong, we take things into our own hands and make the punishment fit the crime. Everything we do wrong in this life will be added to our death. When you make the decision to take life from someone else, you take life away from yourself. The way you see judgment for someone else due to their behavior is the same judgment you call for yourself. That is why you are warned to "treat people the way you want to be treated." We cause this world to be the way it is today. It doesn't have to be this way, but we make the ***choice*** to live this way. We **don't** have to **live in sin**, but sin seems to be much easier for us, so we continue to live that way on a continuous basis. There are people in this world that are so caught up in believing that they are in control, that they don't understand they are part of the cause of so much destruction in this world. We can "all" help to save many lives and cause so many miracles to happen on a daily basis, but we don't have enough ***faith***. ***God*** wants to give us so much peace during our storms, pain, and our hurt, but we don't have the "**Faith**" that He is looking for. We don't acknowledge the true reason for ***Christ*** coming back for us. We ought to **be more like Jesus;** have the ***faith*** and **don't doubt** or question your power. You have a purpose, so **seek God** for your direction. We are given the same instructions that Jesus was given; "live to save and die to rejoice." If you don't help to save someone else, you definitely can't save yourself. It is easy to **praise and bless God** during your sunshine, and hard to do during the rain, but if you hold on to ***God's love*** for you, He will bring you through. You may pray for someone you love to stay away from death and it may not end up the way you prayed, but if you believe and you have faith, **don't give up on God** because He knows what's best for you. You already know that ***God*** didn't promise us eternal life "here on earth," but did it ever dawn on you that there may have been a greater purpose for the reason that your prayers weren't answered the way you called? You can stand over someone's bed that is being called from death and you can ***pray*** for them, but if you don't truly believe and **have total faith** in your prayer for what you are asking, ***God*** can't hear you and your prayer can go unanswered, therefore, **death cannot be stopped**. Your ***faith*** is the activation to your prayer, but what if that person was given an opportunity during their coma stage to either leave right then and there to get to their **promised land**, **or** go back to the **God forsaken world** and "possibly" lose it all? What would be your choice? Yes, you would want to come back, but if ***God*** was to tell you that you and your family's ***faith*** is what will keep them protected and they will be alright without you because you have taught them well enough to trust Him; would you let go then? You have to dig deeper to understand what is really going on? Their death is a wake up call for someone else, but we are so blinded by our troubles and heartaches and pain caused by death. When devastation comes, it is not because ***God*** is punishing us, but because **Jesus came to save** us. Do you think that maybe sometimes we have to let go and take advantage of our last chance at eternal life? I say "sometimes" because not everyone has to let go, and they do make a full recovery with a chance to come back and turn their life around to **do**

God's work. Will they straighten out their life and do what is right, or will they go back to their old ways? Through it all, we need to know that our days are already numbered regardless of what is going on in the world today. Do you know what to believe? It is totally up to you to go and verify everything that you are taught. Live your life to the fullest through ***Christ Jesus.*** Only ***God*** can put you in Heaven or Hell.

When you call someone's name out for the "altar" prayer, **God will** go see about that person in time of need and let them know that someone is looking out for them. He will allow a close call or near death experience to occur just so they can acknowledge Him when He spares their life or abruptly stops an accident from happening. This is an example of our prayers being answered when we don't even acknowledge what has happened. We will talk about it and admit that someone is watching over us, but we don't take it seriously or really know the truth. How many people will truly understand what just happened or even recognize it? Will the person who called out their name at the altar call even acknowledge that fact when they hear about the experience? There is so much we don't take the time to understand so that we may **acknowledge** the real purpose about **life and death**. We do a lot of things **in the name of** "**Jesus**" and don't truly grasp what we are doing. We continue to act on what we know best to do. Some of us take our answered prayers for granted. The first sign should be enough to make you want to change your life and start trusting and believing in ***God***. When you don't acknowledge the message behind your experience the first time, ***God*** will still send another spirit in human form to inform you that it was **a sign from God** for you to come to Him. How many of us hear that message time and time again and truly ignore it? How many times do we hear someone tell us that "***God*** is trying to tell you something?" How many times do you hear "that was nothing and no one but ***God***?" ***God*** makes so many attempts to try to reach out and connect with you, but you continue to turn your back on Him with a deaf ear. He gives your wisdom and knowledge, so why don't you understand?

Chapter 9
Your Heart And Your Mind

In our lives, our hearts should control our minds, but we allow our minds to take over our hearts. The things we choose to believe should come from the heart. When we seek or feel with our heart, we know that there is a good feeling of love or hate. Our mind takes over and dictates what our heart feels. When you think about it and take a good look at the big picture there is only one choice of every decision that you make. Every decision deals with either good or bad. You either have **love** from **God** which is good, or have **hate** from **Satan** which is bad. Only you can decide how you're going to live your life. To live with love in your heart and hate in your mind is a bad combination headed for self-destruction. You cannot live both and be successful in life. In order to truly understand the purpose of our belief and why it is so important for us to have, we must understand the reasoning behind the logic of the fact that ***God*** works with our heart and ***Satan*** plays with our mind. Your heart and your mind are the most important parts that distinguish the characteristics of who you are. The ***Spirits of the Universe*** controls both. The more important of the two is your heart, which is controlled by ***God***. When **God gave** you breath, it gave your heart a beat. When He gave you breath, it was given for a choice to either live or die, both being eternally. He keeps your heart beating to keep the "***blood of Jesus***" flowing through your body. ***God*** has filled your heart with many features to help keep you happy and healthy. The heart is what keeps you alive and breathing. Your body cannot function without the heart; you have a soul with no life. Your heart is filled with ***unconditional love*** for perfect peace and harmony. The heart gives you a sense of feeling to let you know when something is wrong or right in your life. When you speak from ***your heart***, it tells no lies. Your heart is the light that shines within you. The beat of your heart allows your brain to activate your senses. Your heart lets you know when someone or something is not good for you; we just choose to ignore it so we can do what "we" want to do. When your heart feels a touch of sadness from someone doing you wrong, it immediately picks up that bad vibe. Your heart lets you know that you are doing too much, and when it's ok to precede with your activities. Your heart will shut down when something enters the body with contamination. Your heart feels when there is love in the air. Your heart is what allows you to love and hold onto something. When ***the Word*** is ministered to you, it goes straight to your heart for feeling, and then it connects with your mind which makes a decision to either accept the information or decline it. It is very important that you be careful and mindful of the data you collect and allow to enter into your mind. You arc at peace when you follow your heart. When you follow your heart, you make wiser choices out of sound judgment. When you **follow your heart, you can never go wrong** because Jesus is right there to direct and lead the way, "**if**" you let Him. He can't take you anywhere if you don't follow.

Satan controls your mind "if" you let him. Your mind is so easily distracted; open and free to receive just about anything. It is easily influenced by the smallest detail. ***Satan*** cannot get to your heart, that's why he messes with your mind. **Your heart controls your mind** once you understand the concept of your purpose in life. Your heart can take your mind to a place that is so peaceful and harmonious while holding a constant smile on your face to where you just feel good all over. All it takes is that one little bug in your ear that sends a signal to your brain and changes your whole attitude and affects your heart in the worst kind of way. Just that fast you made a transition from the waves that traveled from your mind to your heart and shut off your happy valve. Satan gives you all kind of thoughts and ideas of evil things to do. He will tell you things that sound so good and even point out some examples to make you "***think***" it is ok to do wrong. He will exploit the fact that everybody is doing it; so why not you? ***Satan*** will put something so evil and corrupt in your mind and turn it around to make it appear to be holy. Satan does know the ***Bible*** inside and out. In your mind is a place filled with darkness and sadness, and anywhere there is darkness, that's where you will find Satan. It is not the individual doing the acts; it is the ***evil Spirit*** they choose to activate. In your mind **Satan fills your head with lies** that make you feel that you're not worth the life you live. He is so good that he makes you do all kind of evil vindictive things and then turn them around on you to make you blame yourself to the point you want to commit suicide. Satan puts blinders over your eyes before you go somewhere so you don't see the truth, and then removes them once you get to where you're going so all you see is the fun part of it. He tells you not to believe what is written in the ***Bible*** so you will miss out on the truth. You heard the expression, "**follow your first mind.**" That is a saying because the first time you think of something, it is the spirit of the heart speaking to you, but then along comes the enemy ***Satan*** speaking to your mind and persuade you to do otherwise. That's why we always "regret not following our first mind." There is a constant battle that is going on to help us to either live for the goodness from ***God*** or the evilness from Satan. When we allow our hearts to change to what is on our minds, we block ***God*** from doing His work in us and give Satan all of our attention by allowing him to play on our minds. ***God*** is already in your heart, and His Spirit is the soul in your body, so let Him give you **peace of mind**.

When you read and think about the difference between the heart and the mind, it should open your eyes to the truth of who wants you to be happy and who wants you to self-destruct. Our hearts and minds are what keep us from accepting our own beliefs. There are many reasons why we should believe these facts, but we refuse to see or listen to them. We may all have our own beliefs of how we see things and what we accept to be true, but in the end, our beliefs are about the same thing. That one thing is the "fact" that ***God*** is our Father, and He sent His Son ***Jesus*** to save us. If you believe in ***God***, there is "no" excuse for not believing in ***Jesus***. In the end, there will be no exceptions to that fact if you don't choose to trust and believe in Him now. You can only get to the Father through the Son. The sad feeling about this fact is that you don't have to believe it, but you will regret it. Our acceptance of our beliefs comes from the choices we make, which also affects our lives in some form, shape, or matter depending on the situations in our lives. Our choices will either make us or break us, and that's why it is extremely important to **use your heart** when making decisions. Your belief is very important because it determines the end of your life. After **God gave us breath** and was proud of His creation, He left us with a choice of our own to make to either live with ***Christ*** or die with ***Satan***. All of our choices boil down to one point of being something good or bad. Everything we deal with is either good or bad. Some examples of what are good and bad: we have money, people, music, houses, neighborhoods, food and medications. These are just a few to show how we make a choice in what we will deal with. No one wants to go to a bad neighborhood or eat bad food or take medications that are bad for them, but out of the others, we will contemplate on whether we should accept bad money, hang out with bad people or listen to bad music. Things are labeled as something bad to keep you away from it, but we allow ourselves to be influenced for acceptance of these things by making excuses of how it will benefit us. We know that we should stay away from the bad things in our life because they can cause all kind of problems for us, but it seems like we are so adapted to the evil things in this world, and we can't help but to associate ourselves with these things even though it causes bad things to happen to us. The knowledge and wisdom is out here for us to learn. **God sends** it in all different kind of forms. You have to know when He is speaking to you. It opens your eyes and points out the things that He wants you to know or do, but you don't know it at that time because you want what "you" think is best for you. This is the feeling that you have in your heart when you come across something that you have to make a decision for.

When you sit back and fight and struggle with things that are in your heart to do something for yourself or someone else and you don't do it, you always see the end result of the reason why you should have done what you were feeling. That is **God** trying to teach you how to recognize when He is communicating with you; by showing you the end result of what you were called upon to do if only you would have followed your "first mind" as they say. **God speaks to you** through your heart, but you can only hear Him if you have a live connection with Him. To have that connection, you must have a relationship with His Son ***Jesus***, who is in you. Don't have just any kind of relationship, but have a spiritual one. ***God*** doesn't hear "your" voice, but only that of His Son ***Jesus*** who speaks on your behalf. We can all **talk to God** on our own level and feel that we have a relationship with Him, which is all fine and dandy, but He watches "everything" you do. If you feel that you can talk to ***God*** and do a little here and a little there and it is going to count for something big, you are sadly mistaken. A little here and a little there doesn't pile up to be much and neither will your blessings. ***God*** wants you to do a total 360-degree change for Him, and not for anyone else other than yourself. ***God*** is trying to reveal Himself to you on a daily basis, so open up your heart to Him and let Him do what He's going to do for you. Yes, **God gives** you wisdom, knowledge and a brain to think with, but if you think too long, you will go wrong. So try to follow your heart more because that is where **God is**. You will know when something is of ***God*** because it will feel good and you won't have to think twice about it. Don't look for what's on the outside, but what's on the inside. Just don't try to start living that way until you get that relationship with the Father above, because if you don't have that bond you will run into all kind of problems and issues. Do you believe what is in your heart or what is on your mind? Your belief is what determines your ***faith***. Make sure your choice of belief is one that you won't live to regret. This choice determines your presence and your future. Let's forget about how, what and who we were yesterday and concentrate on who and what we want to be today. Take your time and weigh your options. ***God*** has chosen a path of happiness for you, so why don't you do what is on your mind right now and open your heart up to let ***God*** come in and show you the directions. ***Jesus*** is in you waiting to make that connection with His Father so He can lead the way. All you have to do is let ***Jesus*** lead you to where you need to be so you can do the things that need to be done.

Chapter 10
What Happened To The Church?

Wives and ***women*** of the ***church***, who are not sure of yourselves, it's time to stop being intimidated by these other women coming into the churches and around your neighborhoods dressed a certain way. That woman has the right to go wherever she pleases to, and be around whoever invites her. She may have been called to come to the church to be delivered from her sins. **God says** come as you are. I know we can't blow the command out of proportion, but it is better to have them come to be delivered and saved, then for them to return back on the streets the way they came. She is a "lost" sheep trying to find her way home, and if you are a sheep of Christ, then you should be one to help her find her way. Maybe she's coming around seeking something and maybe she's not, but if you're **tak**ing **care of** and doing what you're supposed to do at **home** with your man or your husband, and you **have** enough **faith in God** to **trust** that man, the least of your worries should be that this woman could come in and disrupt what you have. Instead of turning her away or looking down on her, you should stand your rightful place and be a sister she can call on, or a sister in ***Christ*** to help her along the way. Don't sit and snare and whisper gossip, but instead pull her to the side after the service and talk with her. Ask some questions to try and find out what is going on in her life and what you can do to help her. Give her a hug and let her know that you love her as **Christ loves** His own, but be faithful and honest about it. Let her know that she has come to the right place and is still loved "in spite of." Don't pass judgment on her by what you see without knowing the full truth about who she is. What makes you any better than her? She is human just like you and capable of making mistakes just as you do. You never know what ***truth*** *lies* within her to explain why she appears the way she does. You didn't always **do the right thing**, nor did you always take the right road or steps in the right direction, but someone was there to help you along the way whether you wanted them to be there or not. Some of us still remain to be the same way before accepting ***Christ*** into our life. We don't know how to make a change because we constantly walk around with our noses tooted in the air with the attitude that nobody can tell us anything.

When a female comes to your ***church*** or around your neighborhood, she should feel welcomed with ***open arms***, love, and support. If she comes to your church and doesn't stay for the whole service or never comes back, then that should give every member in that congregation something to worry about. If someone comes to your neighborhood and doesn't come back and they report bad news of it, you should check your backyard for skeletons. This is an indication that someone didn't do their job effectively when Christ was reaching out to them. Believe it or not, that report will be recorded in your book. Our jobs as **servants** for the ***Lord*** **should** be **done** **constant**ly, and it should be done **wherever** we go. **Never miss** an opportunity to show ***Christ*** to one another. You never know when He is presenting Himself to you. If we could get over ourselves and recognize that people come to get help so they can be made right, then we can **position ourselves** to be used as a blessing in their life and help them make the change they're looking for, instead of turning them away. Not every woman dressed that way is coming for attention or for your man. She may be crying out for attention to cover up her pain from lack of love or feeling misfit. If she can't even **turn to the Church**, who else is there for her to turn to? When you feel like someone is trying to take your place or feel your shoes, your jealous tendencies are activated and show everyone just how insecure you are and how little "**faith**" you have in what ***God*** has brought together. When ***God*** brings two people together, there may be feelings of jealousy and skepticism, but their faith in ***God*** will secure those actions from being released. The worst of what you bring out is the doubt to what "you" thought or believed in enough to marry that man. Stand up and **be more Godly** women, then worldly women. You can make a difference if you put someone else first other than yourself. Dig in and get to the root of the problem instead of being judgmental. Let them know that you are there for them, and that they always have a place to come to when they are feeling down. When someone comes to you with a problem they are dealing with or a situation that may have just occurred, you ought to set some time aside to help them because they are sent to you for a reason. Don't push them away or tell them to come back later. There may not be another opportunity or chance for you to help that person. That could be your last test, or their last chance to get it right. As they say, "don't put off tomorrow what you can do today." Let them hear the words "**Jesus loves you**." That is what your responsibility consists of as servants of the ***Church***, and being women of ***Christ***.

For the ***men*** and ***husbands*** of the ***Church***, you need to **step up** and take your rightful place and do what **God** has sent and **commanded you** to do. **Be** more **serious** about His works. Stop using the lame and tiring excuse that a man is a man while trying to convince yourself and the world that, "this is how men are." You are proving society's belief that all men are dogs. We know that "all" is not true, but you make it very hard to believe otherwise. **That is** how "**man**" is, and "man" is **of the world**. That's not how ***God*** created you to be; you were created for a ***greater purpose***. He created you first in the world as an image of Himself to carry on the legacy of His ***goodness*** and His ***grace***. If you **claim** to be of **Christ**, then you need to **represent** yourself as being so. Young men are coming to Church to get filled with the Holy Spirit, and you need to be a role model for ***Christ***. Teach them how to become honorable men that they can be proud of. Not all of them are with the streets; they just imitate and do what they see others do because they don't know who they truly are. Help them to understand the hard knocks of life and how it can affect them long term. Give and show them a reason to want to change their lives. Let them hear how serious it is to get to **know Christ** and how their life can be renewed by trusting in the Lord. Take them and say a prayer with them for ***God*** to use you to reach out and touch their souls. They deserve a chance for someone to help them just as you did. You can help save the young if you make yourself useful by being a positive father figure to them. Most of them don't have a father that they can turn to, and that's where you should be stepping in. Men can find more time to apply to helping young men become men if they stop watching all this temptation out here. There are women all over the world to help you prove just how strong you really are. When you come into ***Christ***, it's not a game anymore of how many females or numbers you can get by the end of the night. It's now time to represent yourself as being an honorable, strong and respectable man. ***God*** has equipped you to carry out these characteristics within yourself. When you become a man **of Christ**, you should no longer be representing yourself or men of the "world," but everything of a real ***Christian*** man. If you are not sure of what a real man is supposed to be like, just go to chapter 16 of this book. Help to teach these young boys and men to realize that this life is not just about the streets and women. ***God*** is using you to guide them and show them direction from getting out of the streets and into a legal career. Talk to them about the factors of the truth behind the purpose of jail cells and funeral homes. Teach them about the real purpose of having a gun in your possession. Be an example of what it means to have other men in your corner for support. Let them know how important it is for children to have their father's in their lives, especially little girls. Show them that "hate" is just a word used to put separation between two or more people because of lack of love. Explain to them that we are brainwashed to learn to hate each other to stop us from succeeding in unity. Let them know that with love and unity, we can conquer the world. Make sure that they understand that the street-life is the quickest way to lose their life forever.

We need more men to be examples of how a man is supposed to treat a lady with respect, but not get caught up with the females that Satan uses to distract us from doing the right thing. Just because a woman walks by you or brushes past you, that doesn't mean that you have to give her the satisfaction of watching her or flirting with her with your eyes and your smile. You don't have to disgrace her just to let her know that the way she is carrying herself is not the way for a woman to act or dress. You can show her that you are a respectable man only attracted to respectable women, and then treat her as though she was your own daughter. Help to teach them how to become young ladies and women that they can grow to ***love***. Yes, she may be beautiful and even sexy, but are not those the same qualities you were supposed to have found in your own wife or woman? Does the looks of her body or the way she walks change what your wife or your woman is supposed to mean to you? Just because she's smiling at you and showing you some attention, does that change what your wife or your woman does for you? Does it change how she makes you feel? Is it that easy for someone to just walk right in and break up what you have already claimed to make you happy? Do you not recognize "***temptation***" when you see it, which is one of the greatest meanings for "***sins***" of the world? Did you not make a vow to **cherish**, **honor**, **love**, and **respect** your wife through sickness and in health; through good and bad till death do you part? Did you not listen to the words "let **NO** man take away what ***God*** has joined together?" Did you not stand before ***God*** and many other witnesses and proclaim those words? If you cannot be trusted before ***God*** with your own words, then who amongst you in the world shall trust anything you say or do to be true? It was you who found that woman and asked her to marry you. It is written, "A man who finds himself a wife, has found a good thing," not a woman who finds a husband. You can find that in **Proverbs 18:22.** **Men** step up to **be men** and "**Imitating Fathers**" **of Christ**, because we only have one true ***Father***. The bigger problem is that we get hooked up with men and women of the "world" and don't take time to **seek Christ** about our **relationships** to make sure that they are sent from ***God***. We accept things not of goodness or ***Christ***, so we are thrown off course and our path of righteousness for true happiness, and so we settle for less than what we deserve. Although you will still endure issues, the bigger ones won't be present because you know he or she is **a true** man or woman of **Christ**. A true **relationship** only **works** when one's ***love*** is true, and that love is only true when you have fully accepted ***Christ*** in your life. It doesn't matter what that person looks like or do, as long as they are in Christ, you will be truly happy. A true man or woman of ***Christ*** that is in a relationship will talk their differences out and then take their problems to ***God*** and let Him work it out for them. **God** is the "only" one who can and **will**, for we "can't" **do** anything without ***Christ*** and expect it to work. If you feel and believe that you can do it all alone; just take a trip down memory lane to the journey of your past and see how many things have actually worked out for you, and how many of them are still going strong to this day. I'm sure after you **seek the evidence**, you will see why you are still in the same position. That is because you are not one with the Father. Remember, this may not apply to everyone, but ***we all*** need to search and look deeper into our hearts and souls. Our present and the future is a reflection of the things we did in our past.

Pastors and Deacons and other active members of the Churches, you are representing the ***Father***. The "One" who you claim to have called you to be in the position you hold. I don't under what would make one step down from their positions **led by God**. What is this issue with a child of ***God*** stepping down because he or she can't do the work anymore? How can you stand in front of many and claim that ***God*** has called you to do this particular ministry and proclaim that you will work for the ***Lord***, and then later on down the line come back and tell people that you are resigning or however you choose to bring it forth? I don't believe that someone should step up and say that they are answering **God's calling** on their life and not take it "very" seriously. If you know that **God is calling**, I don't think you should answer if you are not sure, especially when you know that you are not ready. Other than ***God***, you are the only one who knows what is in your heart. You know that your life has to change when you answer. You have to represent all of the goodness that ***God*** has to offer for you. That means you have to change "all" of your ways to **allow God** to work through you and for you. Don't let anyone stop you from doing what you are called to do. If you are a Pastor, then that means you are in control of and responsible for the Church. If you are a Deacon, then you are under the Pastor's wing and should honor whatever the Pastor decides as long as it is in the **Will of God**. When you accept a position to do work in the Church, you should recognize that you are an assistant to the Pastor. It is your responsibility to make sure that everything you do is in line with the Pastor's intended purpose to bring unity unto that Church. Our purpose for doing work in the Church is to work "together," not "against" each other. The purpose for the gift of ministries that we have is to come together to prepare for the "Coming of our Lord." **God offers** so many great things for you when you make your life about Him and do His will. How can you walk away from all of that? What is it in the "world" that is so important that you would give up on what **God** has **called you** to do? What is wrong with change? When you do something that is in line with ***God's will***, everything will go right in your life as long as you stay with Him. When you accept this position, you show the world what ***God*** is doing in your life and how happy and excited you are. Because others see you and the change ***God*** has made for you, others can now seek change in their own life. You show them that if **God can** do it for you, He can and will do it for them. When you step down from that position, you show everyone how you just gave up on ***God***. You give them the idea that it is hard to do ***God's will***; otherwise you would still be in the same position doing what you were called to do. You just threw your ***faith***, ***trust*** and ***belief*** in the Lord out the window. They see the fact that you were once happy and now you are given up on ***God***, so ***God*** must have stopped working for you, so why would they want to do anything for ***God*** just to be let down. They see the end result of "your" failure, and they fear seeking ***God*** for direction over their life. That's only because they don't understand that it is the individual that gives up because they have lost their faith, and not that ***God*** has walked away from that person. You affect a lot of people when you step down, and ***God*** doesn't take that lightly at all. You have just caused many to give up on their ***faith***. It's not about "I couldn't do it" or "I wasn't ready like I thought I was," because ***God*** is with you every step of the way, and He's not going to call you without preparing you. To turn your back on ***God*** and give up on everything that He has equipped you with, is a "***Hell***" of a price to pay. Before you think about answering ***God's*** calling on your life, it would be wise for you to talk it over with ***God***, not man. Ask Him for direction in that path you are attempting to follow, because your life is about to change completely from old to new. You will have new everything in your life. Everything in between your feelings and your friends will become new. I'm not saying that you should get rid of your old friends, but they should be renewed from your presence and new ones should be added. One thing that can be guaranteed through all of your obedience is that ***God*** will find favor over you and yours. It's definitely worth it.

People of the Church today make it hard for others to want to get right because they are just pretenders. Their worship is playtime for them. They sit around and shout "amen" and praises that are not sincerely from the heart. They want to be something they can't because their heart is not in it, and when your heart isn't in something, it is not true and definitely not real. For this reason, I didn't start this paragraph by saying "members." Churchgoers are in the Church claiming to be a member of the **body of Christ**, but yet and still they will walk right past their own members as though they don't exist. They are too busy on Sunday after service to make sure they speak to, hug, or shake a member's hand. We should feel the love from every member of that ***Church*** to remind each other that we are still there. How can you claim to be a part of the body of ***Christ*** with this kind of attitude? Sunday is a day of Sabbath and we should be resting in Jesus' name for what our Father has done for us, but if something "has" to be done, then by all means get it done. This is the day of the ***Lord*** and we should "all" be celebrating the victory over our lives. We should give Him all the **Honor**, **Glory** and **Praises** for the last six days that He has not been resting because He was taking care of "our" needs. He spends "all" of His time helping you through your day and taking and answering prayer requests and you can't even find the time to stick around just in case He needs you. If you are rushing what ***God*** is trying to do, how can the Holy Spirit reach each body it is sent to? If we take more time and **let God** use us for "His" will to be done, by letting the spirit move in the Church and don't stop until it is done, maybe more of the members would be more sincere about their worship. I would rather see ten dedicated and faithful members, than a whole congregation of members who are hypocritical phonies. Dedicate your life to ***God*** not to the world. **God is** not **watching** you for who you are, but for what you do.

Chapter 11:
The Test Of Temptation

I would like every man and woman reading this to think about the paragraph before this one. Think about the word "**temptation**." As I stated, this is one of the greatest meanings to committing sins in the world. Everything that comes our way that ***attempts*** to take the place of our happiness is a **test**. If you are in a relationship and you are happy, it is ***Satan's*** job to come and try to destroy it, so he will send one of his finest, sexy walking, sexy talking women/men with a built out of this world, just to show you how ***weak*** you are. The same goes with if you have a house, a car, or a job that you are content with and keeps you satisfied, ***Satan*** will send someone around you with a better house, car, and a better paying job, and have them boasting, just to give you reason to feel jealous or envious. Don't you know that's just **Satan's way** of keeping you from moving up to the next level? We all have to start somewhere to **show God** that we can handle what we have, before we can elevate to the next level. The first thing we do is knock what that person did to get what they have, or start feeling "why don't I ever get a break like that!" That **is a test**! Don't you know that **Satan asks God** for His permission **to tempt you**? Yes, even Satan can ask and receive. Don't forget that he was one of ***God'***s angels before he failed. Understand the word "***tempt.***" Satan can't make you do anything; **it is your choice**. When **God gives** him permission, He is basically giving **His all** for you, trusting and believing that you are going to **pass the test**. **God knows you** are His child and that you have enough faith not to let Him down, because you know that after this test is over, your ***reward*** is going to be so much greater because you trusted and believed in Him enough to **avoid Satan's temptations**. **God loves you "in spite" of** and gives you the benefit of the doubt by trusting that you will stand up to Satan because of your trust in Him, but here you go with your weak spirit, unbelieving, always complaining flesh, and let the devil's works take over. That was your opportunity to **let the light** inside of you **shine** and **Glorify God's** goodness through your **testimony** of His undying love for you. These kinds of failures give ***Satan*** the opportunity to be able to smile and run his mouth to ***God*** about how; "I told you he or she would give up on you when they have what they want. They get too happy and so comfortable with what they have that they forget where it came from. They expect you to help them every time, and when you don't, they think you don't exist. How foolish of them! They don't understand anything about ***faith***. **They don't read** enough of **your Word** on their own time. **They don't** have that **bond**ed relationship with you. They think you are the one toying with them, so **they come to me** without missing a beat; figure that one out. **They turn on you** without a care in the world. They don't know how to let the storm past and let you help them through it. They don't know how to experience the works of other people's testimonies. I knew they didn't ***trust*** you or ***believe*** that you were right there. They don't understand the purpose of their own life because they think it's about them. Those are the ones **I love**, and that's why I come to **you** about particular ones; I see them as a failure because they don't care about their life anyway." This is what Satan banks on your life, and with most of us, he always wins. Another soul sent to the back of the never-ending **wait**ing line **for another test**. Yes, Satan does have conversations with ***God*** about you and your weak flesh. When you ***have faith***, things don't always come when you want it. ***God*** allows you to go through hard times so others can see the things you're going through, and the ***strength*** you receive from it. You have to go through something in order to come out stronger. This is the time ***God*** permits Satan to tempt you to give up on ***God***, and all you have to do is stand by your ***faith***, ***trust***ing and ***believ***ing that ***God*** is getting ready to move in your life. If you don't **have faith** and **believe** in **God's Word**, what do you have left to stand on? This is when **Satan sends** his warriors out **to destroy** your hopes and dreams, but only **if you let them**. They will come around and keep talking about the things you're going through, "telling you how they feel sorry for you, how they would hate to be in your shoes, you are going down, and this situation doesn't look good." They make comments such as, "don't you pray to ***God***, when is things going to happen for you?" You need enough witnesses for what ***God*** is about to do for you and through you. You need others in your life to doubt what you **believe** in, otherwise, how can you be a testimony if you don't go through it and stand firm? Let them hear and see you **praise** and thank **God** before you get what you've asked for, so they can understand what happened once the blessings start pouring over. Others need to see that, through all the mess you were going through, you held onto your **faith**, **trust**ed and **believe**d that **God** was about to be glorified through all of your **blessings**. Know that when things seem to be getting worst and you just can't take it anymore, this is because **Satan knows** that your **blessings are on the way**, so he has to do everything he possibly can to make you miss this turn in your life so you will give up on ***God*. Shake the Devil off! God will** surely open up those doors for you for others to see what happens when you are about Him, in ***faith***, ***trust***, and ***belief***. Never let others see you sweat, ***God*** knows your pain and feels your pain. He sees what you're going through. If you **don't let Satan take** anything away **from you**, at the end of the **test**, you get to keep it all with interest and benefits. Now you get to **sit back and enjoy** all the things "you" have accomplished through "**your faith**." Remember, these things only happen because **God** gives you a choice. He doesn't make you do anything, He **only requires** that we **Love** one another and treat each other right. Do you believe that it is fair for you to call on Him only when you need something? Do you think it's fair that when He can't get to you quick enough for your standards you should doubt what He can do for you? You are not the only one going through tough times. You may have just missed your opportunity for a blessing when you were busy basting in your flesh not realizing that He had already answered you, but it wasn't how you expected it to be, so now you have to wait till your turn is up again. Your ***Father*** is "not" a **God** of lies. He **will** do just what you **ask** of **Him**, but are you truly dedicated and ***faithful*** to Him enough that He should just move when you ask Him to? He already told you that **He would supply "all" of your needs**. The rest of what you're asking for is just for your pleasure.

Chapter 12: Where Is Your Dedication?

We need to **be** more serious and **dedicated to** our positions in **the Church,** just as **we need** to be with **each other**. The **Church is** what makes **the body of Christ**. Why are the Pastors playing around in the "pool pit?" Why are "married" Pastors messing around with women in the Church, Bishops sleeping with boys, and Deacons fooling around with worldly women? Why is the First Lady of the ***Church*** running around with other men? What's the deal with adultery? How do you stand up in front of so many people **preach**ing **and teach**ing **the Word**, and you don't even walk what you talk? How can you be an example, if you don't set one? Does the money come before the Lord? Do the material rewards **come before God**? Isn't the love of money the root of **"all"** evil? You get so high and mighty that you forget your position and **who brought you there**. That is the life you chose to give up when you accepted your calling, or was it ***your calling***? Were you "ordained," or "damned?" Where are your morals? You vowed to make a difference; you vowed to **help to change the world**. You are supposed to **be separate from the world**. We should **see the light** shining in you, but we don't see it until the skeletons jump out at us. ***God*** is not the cause of all this mess, but He can bring you out of it. Do you not **believe** what's going to happen on your judgment day, or is there something you have learned in ***Bible*** school that we don't know? You **claim** to love ***the Lord***, but yet and still you continue to do Satan's work. **God** told you through His **Son** that you could only **serve ONE God**. You "cannot" serve TWO. Why do we have to come to Church all fly and jazzy just to **hear the Word**? I'm not saying that it's not ok to move up a level, but is there not something else that could be done with the money? This is part of the reason why we don't take Christ serious, because everything is becoming a big "show and tell." Why not "show and tell" **what God** truly **means to you**. Why do we still have homeless people on the streets? Why are we still feeding the same starving children in other countries, if we have been funding them for centuries? How big are these places that they can't contain food over there? If it only costs seven dollars to send one 50lb box of food to feed the hungry, and we've had many who have funded hundreds of thousands of dollars, where are all of these boxes that they should be able to store for centuries to come? These are the questions we should be asking ourselves while trying to find a resolution for them; not out here disrespecting our Father's purpose. I believe it's written in the ***Bible*** that **God does greater works** for those who take care of the homeless. We come up in the world and fall right back into society's hands. I'm not knocking anyone, but I am speaking the cold-hearted truth.

We all know how hard it is for us to survive out here, but we do want to enjoy some things during our lifetime here. There are a lot of places I would like to go and things I would like to see, but it is so costly anymore. I would like to take all five of my children to see certain plays, but it would cost me more than $200 dollars just to take them all. It's not fair to take one or two and the others stay home, but what can I do? I would like to take them out to the movies so we can have the chance to mingle and meet other people, but that can become costly too. I have a solution to that problem, but it confines me to my home. I know how to wait for the movie or play to make it on video. It doesn't bother me, but it does affect my children. I feel that we should learn to build our own, so that way we can charge what we see to be fit and fair. We can't buy houses in certain areas because we're not wanted. They price the houses at unaffordable prices and tell you that you're not worthy enough because your credit is not good enough. This society is mostly about making money, and they don't care who they knock or keep down to get it. They tell us that there is no discrimination but yet and still on your application they want to know your race. Why is that? What difference does the color of my skin make? We all shed the same color blood and we all are humans. We are so blinded that we can't see what we need to do to save and build on our own. We want to be like everybody else; we want to give a little and keep a lot. The money will not leave with us when we go. **God said** He will take care of all our needs so we can do our part in contributing to those who truly need help. You shouldn't be concerned about what your family will have when you leave from here, because if you truly and sincerely do your part while you are here, there will be no need for worry when you leave. That is having true **faith in God**. He's not going to ask you what you left for your "family," but what did you do and leave for "His family?" It's not meant for us to make it in this world by man, it is meant for us to make it through **Christ** and Christ alone. He is the only **Free Spirit** walking this earth that will bring you your every desire as long as you walk with Him. He will introduce you to everyone you need to meet to make that happen, but you don't trust Him enough and that's why this world is the way it is now. The high and mighty thinks that this is their world and they can do what they want to. It may be that way right now, but in the end is where it truly matters, but by then it will be too late to say "**I'm sorry**." That is a mighty high price to pay just to try and be the boss, especially when none of this stuff belongs to us. It's all here by the **Grace of God**. ***Love*** the money now, because you won't have it in the end, but **you will be punished** for it. I'm not knocking anyone; I'm just speaking some true facts, and if the shoe fits, then wear it. It saddens me to know that these kinds of sinful acts go on inside the church and out in the world. How can you say that you are **stand**ing **for Christ** when you are feeding off of Satan's plate? This just goes to show you that ***God*** does intervene to make us right, "**in spite of**" what we do, but it seems like these folk would rather choose to ignore ***God*** and His true purpose for their lives, just to make some fast cash. How pitiful! Who can we truly **trust? No One but God** will be there for us. We know **He will never leave us, nor forsake us**, and He will never fail you. I am fed up with all of the many things that go on in today's society, and that is the real reason that **I'm here on my own to do God's work**. I am striving to be a true servant for my ***God***. I know I will never be perfect. There is nothing I won't do for Him. I don't care who don't like it, I only ***pray*** that you receive and apply it, because there is **No weapon formed** that shall prosper against me, for **I know** that my **God** is with me. I'm doing my part, and you should do yours. We should all be on the same page when it comes to ***God***. **I love God** with all my heart, mind, body, and soul. I know I'm not the only one who feels this way, nor am I the only one who is serious about ***God's business***, but we need more people to **step up** and take notice to **put the Word out**. There are a lot of things that are important in today's society that we need to handle, but **NOTHING** is more important than **God's Will**.

Why is it that we seem to be living in the beginning of the Old Testament? Everyone who stands to fit the description of these characters, **you are going**

straight to Hell, and you don't even **care about what you're doing to God**. People come to **Church** to **be delivered from** their **sins** and **healed from** their **sickness**, but they can't get it because the **Church** constitutes a bunch of **hypocrites**. People have the nerve to stop and ask ***God*** why He isn't moving in their lives, with all this selfishness and wickedness, why would He? Maybe ask a better question. What am I doing for ***God***? Have you given Him any real reason to reward you? Have you changed the way you walk or talk? Do you have true ***Faith*** in Him? If you don't truly believe that He can and will, why should He? He has already proved His ***Will Power*** and what He's capable of doing, so He doesn't have to show you anything. What if ***God*** thought as much about you as you thought about Him? What percent of the time would He be thinking about you? ***Dedicate*** your life to Him. He has already done it for you.

Chapter 13:
The Tree Of Knowledge

All of these evil signs are that of **Satan work**ing overtime **in our minds** because he doesn't want you and me to do or be right. He doesn't want you on the straight and narrow. He wants to make sure we stay lost and never find out the cold hearted truth. ***Satan*** knows that once you get the knowledge, you are headed in the "right" direction. You have to seek it first to find it. There is nothing "right" about Satan, so why would he want you to get a grasp on what's right about your life? He will do "anything" to keep us from finding the truth. He uses a lot of people out here today to release information out here to go against what the **Truth is**. He doesn't want us to learn and grow from the "**tree of knowledge**." ***God*** has supplied us with this tree of knowledge because it contains so many memories of everything we need to know about Him and our purpose in this life. There is no "bad" fruit upon this tree. Everything that bears on this tree is of something that is full of goodness and truth. You can get fruit from this tree just about anywhere in this world; you just have to be mindful of what is good and what is evil. If you go to ***the Bible*** and get this information, you won't have to worry about anything that is evil. This tree of knowledge stems from the families that have been through "***History***." History is what is in the past regarding knowledge that's been around for centuries, including everything you just learned yesterday. A place you can't go back to, but something you can learn about in the present and apply it to your life for today and the future. The tree of knowledge I'm speaking about is the tree from "**His Story**." This is the story about **Jesus**, the man sent to **bear our sins** upon the cross so that you and I may have ***eternal life***. This should be in your heart. **God planted** good things **in your heart** that consists of **love**, **faith**, **peace**, **joy**, and **happiness. W**hen you mix those together you get abundance, which is the life He promised us, if we choose to live for Him. He didn't promise that life to you if **you remain in** "**sin**." ***God*** doesn't honor sin, nor is He part of sin, and that's why He sent **Jesus** to wash them away. This **is the truth** about ***His Story*** that some people don't want us to know. **We** are all in a sinful world and every last one of us **Need Jesus** in our lives. We have a ***choice*** of how we want our lives to be and what we will make of it. ***God*** doesn't take anything away from us because He promised to never leave us nor forsake us, but we block ourselves from the things given to us by either letting the blessing go or handling in the incorrect manner. In this manner, when the blessing doesn't work how "we" think it should, we walk away from it. He definitely didn't promise us that we would live in this world forever. All of our days are numbered, but ***God*** has the **life** He wants you to live already predestined, but you have to **learn** how to obtain **it**. It's not hard. In **Timothy I 6:17**, **God** tells you to put your hope in Him and He will richly provide you with everything for enjoyment. When we make our lives about ourselves and what we want and how we want it, we put ourselves first, then set out to seek the things we want and how we want to live it; basically you tell ***God***, "I got this." "We" let **God know** "I can handle this," "I know what I want and need, because I know what's best for me," so you start your day to go off sailing through this **world of sin** to get what you want. **You left without God**. Take notice that I didn't say "***God*** left you," but "you left Him." Sounds to me like you're on your own. Oh, and don't forget that when you're by yourself there is no protection around you and ***no light***, so you're in total darkness. Guess whose territory you are in? Satan, the enemy sees you in the dark because that is his world. This is a perfect opportunity for him to grab you to give and show you something that "looks" and "sounds" good. At this point, you would never know one from the other because you are about "self." Notice the words, ***looks*** and ***sounds***. Everything is not always what it looks like, and everything you hear isn't always what it is. But then again, what do you know; you never stopped at the **tree of knowledge!**

Chapter 14:
Victim Of Satan

I have been through a lot in my life since I have become old enough to be out on my own. Some of the examples I have spoken about were part of my life before I truly found and accepted ***Christ*** in my life. I had my share of partying and being with different guys, which was my main issue for my lack of true happiness. I have a big heart filled with a lot of compassion, and I wanted to share my love with someone and make them one of the happiest men around. I had the opportunity with one, but I was not mature enough to see that back then and I let him go. Till this day I have not had the opportunity with someone real and dedicated. I tried to settle down and have just one, but the ones I got involved with were not satisfied with just one woman. I went out to clubs, drinking and smoking cigarettes and weed. I was one who used to smoke cigarettes at the age of fourteen because I thought I was grown and cool. I was one who said I would never stop smoking cigarettes until one day I was shown differently. I had a severe attack of acid reflux. One day my chest and stomach was hurting so bad that I thought I was going to die. I was throwing up for almost twelve hours straight. I'm talking about from twelve in the morning until twelve the following afternoon. I couldn't take it anymore, so I called on ***God*** through His Son ***Jesus*** and prayed that if He would just take the pain away I would promise not to touch another cigarette. My pain was instantly taken away, and as I promised, I never inhaled another cigarette. **Thank God**! It's been about seven years now, and I have not touched a cigarette, but about three years ago I picked up smoking black and milds. They didn't cause pain to me because they were milder than cigarettes, but that was a broken promise although it wasn't cigarettes. I don't smoke them because I feel like they give me relief or they make me calm down, because that would be so far from the truth. I have the strength to not smoke one every day or every other day. I have the will power to stop at any given moment because I am equipped with the strength. There is "no excuse" for why I do it and it's not a habit for me, but I do it just because. That is not my excuse, but that is the "reason" why I do it. This too will pass. My experience with the acid reflux was the first sign to show me that ***God*** was real.

In my relationships I tried to remain faithful with the man in my life at that time, but I became part of the game of cheating after I couldn't take it anymore. Instead of me doing the right thing and walk away, I joined in. That didn't make me any better than them, in fact, that made me ***just like them***. I went through physical and mental abuse with half of my relationships, and I found a way to let them stay around. I had and owned my own home, so the men came and stayed with me. I never had the opportunity to walk away from them. I always had to put them out, which is something I don't like to do to people, but when enough is enough it's time to go. In my relationships, I always gave **100%** of my **love** from the door because I believe in being who I am. I didn't know how to take my time and find out everything there is to know about someone before opening myself to him. I would always be the one to **find the good in someone**, and that's the part of them that I would cling to. I always wanted to be the wife that most men can only dream of, but I never had the opportunity with the right man. By them not being a true man, I didn't get to show that side of me. They knew that I was a good woman, but they didn't know the real woman in me.

My first marriage was with the wrong person because we were not put together by ***God***. This man was never faithful to me since the beginning of the relationship, but something inside of me always felt that anyone could change. I didn't understand at the time that they had to be the one to want to change. I was ***faithful*** to him for the first four years of our relationship of seven years; we were married by the second year. After a while of him cheating and the mental and physical abuse I went through, I couldn't take it anymore. I sat down with him and let him know that I didn't love him anymore and he needed to go so that he wouldn't have to sneak and do the things he wanted to do. He would never leave, not because he honored or cared about the marriage and being a family, but because he wanted to make his life easier for himself. This went on for the remainder of the relationship; me yelling and screaming at him telling him I didn't love him nor was I in love with him anymore, but he refused to go. I finally gave it up and let him know that ***God*** seen what was going on, and one day He would make a way for him to leave, and when that time came it would be all over. My ex-husband fell into **Satan's trap** and the door of opportunity was opened for me to make him leave without a choice. I had put my faith in ***God*** and didn't even understand what I was doing at the time. After my husband left, I was in my mess of flesh doing things that were not of ***Christ***. I was smoking weed on a daily basis. I never tried any other drugs. I was never really much of a drinker once I hit the age of twenty-two outside of a drink or two when I went out every once in a while. I would drink maybe a can of beer here and there at home for the most part. I was not where I was supposed to be.

All four of my daughters were on the stepping and mime team at our Church back at home in Pittsburgh. I wouldn't go to their practices or rehearsals because I had more important things to do. At least that's what I thought, but I didn't realize the more important thing was for me to be there to support my children. My sister Monica was starting to get heavily into ***Church*** and she was on the mime team and was the leader of the step team. I remember how she would pull on me to come into the Church building and tell me how I needed to be there. I would tell her that instead of her forcing me and telling me what I needed to do, maybe she should ***pray*** on it for me and be thankful that ***God*** has moved her in that direction. If she had enough faith, then **God will** do the same for me, but she couldn't make someone do what they don't want to or not ready to do, because that would defeat the whole purpose of their presence. After a while she finally stopped saying anything to me about it. Now I can look back and see that her prayers were answered, but not how she expected them to be. I had an opportunity to leave Pittsburgh, which was something I always wanted to do, so I took advantage of the offer. This was my big break to escape all the drama and get on with my life with this new man, but to my surprise, the reason I thought I was moving was not for my purpose but for someone else. I was moving for one reason, but it turned out to be just the total opposite of what I thought. I was supposed to be moving to start a new life with a man who was coming from Florida and get married, but ***God*** had something else in mind for me. He wanted to get me out of my mess that I was in, so just like the gospel songs speak today, He had to move me away from the people and the things that I loved the most so I could come to Him. The man I came here with had another agenda and plans for another life with someone else. I didn't get mad at this person. Although I felt pain in my heart, I refused to let the situation change the kind of person I was. So I remained to be friends with him, and we stayed together in the same household for the first year because neither one of us knew anyone in this small town of Lumberton, NC. I found me a nice Church to go to about a half hour away from me, after visiting a few others, but ***God*** used my current Pastor to draw me closer to Him and to the Church where I believed He had work for me to do. I still attend that church to this day. My friend didn't believe that ***God*** sent Jesus, nor did he believe in tithing. I would never force my belief on him, but I would give him some scenarios to think about. After a year, he finally starting coming to my church and eventually gave his life to ***Christ***. It was on an Easter Sunday. I didn't feel right living with him anymore, so I felt that it was time for us to separate from under one roof. I didn't realize that was my purpose for being here with him at the time. After that relationship, I figured I would **pray** and **ask God** to send me someone who was dedicated to Him, ***faithful***, ***honest***, ***loving***, ***caring***, and who would be just for me. Not long after my friend left, I met someone else. When I met this man, he informed me that he was a Deacon, and he also told me about the different activities he was involved in at his church. I was also informed about the issues that led to his divorce. He told me everything about what he went through with his wife and how she cheated on him, and all the things he did for her and she never appreciated it. My first question was if he was married, and of course the answer was no. I heard all of that, but I was more into the spiritual aspect of it. I was so excited about finding someone in ***Christ*** that I started falling for him. After he told me he was falling in love with me, I felt like I was in heaven, and ***God*** was about to make magic in this relationship. He would always tell me to put my trust in ***God***. He would give me good advice on how to handle certain situations and would make sure me and my children's relationship was secure. He would tell me to "**walk by faith not by sight**," and he would quote different scriptures to me to help me build up my faith in ***God***. All these good things he was telling and advising me about, and all I could think about was the basis of the relationship and where we were going with it. I couldn't see at the time that ***God*** was using him to get me where I needed to be. He would always tell me to get things in order for my family and me first because he wasn't going anywhere. He would come to visit me from time to time when he would get the opportunity to, and he has met my children and some of my family and friends. All these things sounded so good, but he never opened his doors to me for me to come and visit him at his house or meet his family. I would always reflect back on "walk by faith and not by sight," and make myself believe that this is something different and as long as ***God*** was in the mist of it everything would be ok. I kept my **faith in God** to bring this relationship together the way I thought it was supposed to be. I never rushed for marriage or for us to move in together. I thought I was in love with this man, not because of his looks or his occupation, but because of the spiritual man he was claiming to represent at the time. I honestly thought that my prayers were answered for an honest, dedicated, faithful, and spiritual man. He only lived about 30-45 minutes away, but he never wanted me to take that drive and have my kids on the road just to come and see him. He was a truck driver and I know about all the things I've heard about them, but I believe in giving everyone the benefit of the doubt, so as usual, I found the ***goodness*** in him through his spiritual conversation. He knew how I felt about not coming to see him, but he always had a come back reason of why I couldn't. He had seen so many accidents on the road and he didn't want that to happen to me and mine. Ok, I can understand that one. He got me to believe that he was trying to get his place together and make it suitable for me and my children to come and see him, but that never happened. Our relationship lasted a little over a year, guess what; I still never made it down there. He kept me in the dark, which was an indication that he was not sent by ***God***, because ***God*** doesn't keep us in the dark that's ***Satan***'s job. We never went out on a date, but I did get to go on the road with him. I never asked him for anything unless it was an emergency. He did very little material wise but a lot spiritually, and that's what I was into. His thing was that he was not going to be taken down the same road he went down with his wife when she left him for one of his friends. I am a very good friend to all I come in contact with, and I am a people person. Just about everyone I come in contact with enjoys my company because I love to keep good spirit around. I can talk about anything, but my conversations somehow always involve ***God***. When I moved out here, being that I was single, I met a couple of guys who became just acquaintances. I had no interest in having a serious relationship with them;

it's just that I wanted an opportunity to meet new people through them. I was just looking for some people to get to know the surroundings. I met two within the first year of moving here, one with whom I was working. I stayed in contact with them every blue moon just to see how they were doing, nothing ever happened between us. I am still friends with the same people, but I never met any females because all the ones I would come in contact with were a lot younger than me, and we were on different levels. The women of the church I attend were in their own family circle and I do understand, but I felt like I didn't fit somehow. I never met any females for me to hang out with, so I was more of a homebody and spent most of my time with my children.

Some things happened in this relationship that may have given him indication that he may not have been able to trust me, but I always confirmed my faithfulness and my dedication to one man, and asked him to do the same thing he was asking me to do, **"Trust God**," not man. Everything will come to light. I don't think he believed that. I had to believe that he was miles away and lived alone and he only wanted to be with me, but he didn't do the same thing. He didn't put his trust in **God** to **reveal** the **things** that I was doing. In the end, we both lost our trust in each other, but I believed that ***God*** sent him to me. He claimed that he **prayed to God** and asked Him to remove me from his life if I wasn't the one and every time he called me I was right there. He had already helped me **get** my relationship **right with God**, but for some reason he still didn't open the doors for me, so I pursued my own ways to verify his story. That didn't pan out so well. He got upset and the relationship went down hill from there. He never opened the doors, but I still remained ***faithful*** because I allowed myself to accept the fact that ***God*** was doing something good in my life, and if it wasn't this man, then I knew that ***God*** was preparing me for the one He made just for me. This man just stopped calling without notification or reason, so I had to give up on this man. I still ***pray*** for him and love him as a brother in Christ. Boy! Talking about blinders and wishful thinking! I was way in over my head, but it was an experience that I needed for strength. What **Satan** meant for **evil**, **God** turned it around for **good**.

My acquaintances, including the one I came here with still remains to **be a**

true friend that I can call on if there is anything they can do for me. I had to ask myself, who these men truly were and what did I get out of the relationships. I did get a closer walk with ***God*** by learning how to put my **trust** and ***faith*** in **God** and not in man. I learned that they were not the men **God sent** to be my husband. The flesh part of me would allow myself to feel that these men were "**wolves in sheep's clothing,**" but the ***Spirit inside*** of me helps me to understand that they were the strengtheners during my journey through my Christian walk. **God** used them to help **strengthen me** so I would know how to deal with heartaches and heartbreaks from dealing with men, being that my weakness was men. I have learned how to deal with my feelings for people and how to **be patient** enough so I can get what I truly want. As the saying goes, "the best things come to those who wait."

Of all the things I was feeling, I never understood that ***God*** was opening my eyes to see what to expect when He sends the man He has chosen for me. I didn't agree with a lot of things these men were doing because they were not of ***Christ***, but I thank them for allowing ***God*** to use them. I can't hold myself responsible for what someone else does to me, but only for what I do to others. I didn't know these men's reasoning for doing the things they had done to me, but there was a greater purpose served from the relationships. Rather than for me be a disappointed, bitter, angry, or upset woman, I pray that they create a stronger bond with ***God*** so that they will know how to **make** wiser choices and **Christian decisions** when handling certain situations in their lives, especially when it deals with other people's feelings. Although I was blinded by love in these relationships, I now **see** that **God** was truly doing something amazing in my life. We all have a weakness of something in our life that keeps us from doing what ***God*** has called us to do. We can't stay focused on the things we need to do for ourselves, for giving all of our attention to what weakens us. Being that my "weakness" was men, this was the area in my life that needed to be strengthened so I would learn to put ***God*** first. He showed me how to follow His lead, and everything will come in His time, but on time just the way I want it. He opened my eyes up to recognize what a real relationship where true love comes together is all about. I have learned the difference of knowing when **God sends** something to me and when I get something for myself. I understand what it means to have a bond with **Jesus** so I will know when **God is reaching out** and talking to me. My relationship with ***God*** gets stronger and stronger as I press forward to getting to know Him more and more. I have not given up on love because I know ***true love*** will find me one day. ***God*** is perfecting me for the man He has perfectly created for me. It's not that we will be "perfect" as in we will never do wrong, but perfect enough to be what a "***good***" man and woman wants from and a husband and wife. He or she may not come with good looks and a nice body, but it will be "true love," and that's what is important in a relationship. Most of our life, we miss out on a true relationship because when that "special" someone comes into our life and shows us so much love, we turn them away because they don't have the looks we expected them to have. You just pushed away your blessing in disguise, and now you wonder why you can't find a "good" man or woman to love you. You can't find it the way you want it because love is not something you can see, it is something that you feel. Love is blind, but when ***God*** is in the mist of that love, you see ***Jesus***. This is the kind of love that can't go wrong, as long as you stay in ***Christ***. If He put them together, it's until death do them part, not man. That's when you know that there is no greater love than the one sent to you from up above.

This experience I went through of being a victim of ***Satan*** didn't teach me how to hate, but in fact, it taught me how to love more as well as how to understand the purpose for someone being in my life. I now see that the man ***God*** brought me here to North Carolina with was the one ***God*** used to draw me closer to Him so I can get to know Him, and the one I met after that relationship was the one **God** used for me to **experience** my journey and go through my storms of trials and tribulations to teach me about trust and faith. I strongly believe in treating people the way you want to be treated, and do to others as you would have them to do to you. I had to learn to **put God first** in my life and let everything else come as it was meant to come, and that was after I made the decision to let go and **let God** have His way. I know **God will** allow my hopes and dreams to come true; I just have to prepare myself for it and do His work first. **God** will open your eyes; we just see what we want to see. On this journey I have found **my true love in Christ**; the one that will never leave me. I have also found the woman in me. I have learned how to put my **trust in God** and let Him lead the way and take care of all my problems, while I continue to do His will for my life. I don't regret anything about my journey because ***God*** knew what He was doing, and it strengthened me and made me a better and stronger ***Christian***. I no longer shed tears from what someone do to me, but from what they do to ***God***. I also shed tears because of what ***God*** has done for me, to me, and through me. I am grateful and so thankful to Him. If you don't have that relationship with ***God***, you will never understand where I am coming from right now until you have that bond. Getting to know Him is the best feeling I have ever had in my whole life.

Chapter 15:
How To Soften Your Heart

When you first **accept Christ** into your life, it will be the beginning of your relationship with ***God***. When you get to know Jesus, you are ready to start your journey for change in your life. When you start reading the Bible and talking to ***God***, you will "become" a changed person. You are becoming more and more like ***Christ*** and you can now go out and do the works that you are created and called to do. At this point, you understand **God's purpose** for your life because you can hear Him more clearly. I only gave a small detailed part of my life, not to be noticed or recognized, but so you can see that I have had my share of bad experiences without ***Christ*** in my life. I wanted to share my experiences with you because **I love God** with all of my heart and soul. I am stronger and wiser. I wanted to open your eyes up to some true testimonies and real stories of issues we all deal with on a daily basis so you can see that I am no different from you. I want you to know that you are not the only one going through some rough times. It happens to the best of us. ***We all*** make bad choices from time to time, but everything will be just fine if you just **put it in God's hands** and ***trust*** and ***believe*** that He will work it out. These experiences are part of life, and that's what makes us stronger. The things I have been through and how I came out of them is what made me answer when **God called** me. If you make your life about ***God***, He will make His business about you. I wanted you to see that just because we pray and ask for something, that doesn't mean we will get it the way we want it. Your blessing may not come in the form that you pray for it, but it will serve the purpose in which you prayed for it. Use the blessing for the purpose in which it was sent. Don't waste it or take advantage of it, because it will be passed on to someone else who will be more deserving of it. Why does it take for you to lose something before you can see how beneficial it was to you? If you are not sure what to do with the blessing, seek ***Christ***. You also need to know that when you are going through something that is considered an emergency to you, if you are just willing to **let God** know how serious you are by offering a sacrifice to Him, He will **work** instantly **for you**. You may need to make an offer, because it may not be your time for a ***blessing***, but because you have made a sacrifice to our merciful ***God,*** He will move quickly for you. We can't get our blessings the way we want them until **God knows** that we are truly ready for it. *God* knows our hearts and what we can handle. He knows what is right for us as well as what is best. Here is an example of how your prayers can be answered; if **God sees** that you can't even manage ten dollars, and you ask for one thousand; why would He give you that much and you can't even handle ten dollars. He may give you one hundred dollars to see how you manage that, just because you have asked and He is a **merciful God**. When ***God*** sees that you are sincere and ready for what you are asking, He will give it to you just how you have asked for, just like He did for Moses. You can verify that in **Exodus 33:17**. ***God*** speaks through each and every one of us to reach out and help the next individual. He comes to speak to you individually, but He does it through the human body. So, if you are not careful and don't listen to other people when they come around you, you will miss out on what ***God*** is trying to tell you. ***God*** will even use your enemy to answer you.

Every time I think back on my past, I get more insight on what not to do as well as how to handle certain situations. I now realize that if I had not gone through these storms, I wouldn't be where I am today. I am amazingly happy at what my ***God*** has done for me and through me. I don't feel foolish or stupid for what I have been through or for what I have experienced, because it takes personal experience to actually appreciate what you have learned to apply towards your future. I truly feel so blessed to know what I know today, because not all of my experiences were bad. There were more good experiences than bad; besides it allowed me to be an example of how you can bounce back through ***Christ***. I want the people who have a loving and compassionate heart that is filled with unconditional love, to know that you don't have a reason to feel ashamed, foolish, stupid, or used just because **you chose** to open up your heart and show someone love and they chose to take advantage of it. You are only being you and don't ever let anyone change you or stop you from being that loving person. **God sees everything** and He will send the right person to you that will give you everything you deserve. There are people out here that are cruel, greedy, and all about themselves and what they can get out of the deal. What can those who are full of these evil characters possibly give or contribute to society that would be positive? We can all relate to each other's storms, so there is no reason that we shouldn't be out here helping and listening to one another. Let's stop judging other people and their situations as though we don't cause ourselves to go through situations. No "one" body is better than the next. We all go through the same struggles in life, which is to draw us closer to ***God***. Stop putting each other down and **show more unconditional love**. Learn to contribute more of your time that you "waste" doing nothing, and apply it towards someone else's time that can really use it to help strengthen their life. It's easy to sit back and read someone else's book and pass judgment, but when was the last time you read your own and examined it? Most of you will find the author to be very confused. Observe and correct your own faults and downfalls before pointing out someone else's. Not too many people in this world today are out to truly help someone else. They just come around and ask questions about what is going on in someone's life just to be in someone's business so they will be able to gossip. Most of them are steady looking for a way to make money for them self instead of trying to find a way to help someone else. I am not passing judgment on how people are, but I am only speaking the truth about how they live. Look forward to being a blessing in someone's life instead of a stump and block. I have been through some of the same things, but I don't like the way any of our actions cause pain to ***God***. **I am fed up** and I am tired of the way this world is, and so is our ***Heavenly Father***. There is too much killing, stealing, and hatred going on in this world today. People are really killing people over money and territory that do not belong to them. This world is all about making money to do evil things, and that will be the main reason for majority of this world being condemned to ***Hell***. I speak out because I care and I do not wish any of this on my worst enemy. We need to stand up and make a difference in return for Jesus the same way He has stood up and done for us. Let's be more serious about doing service for ***God***. For as much as He does for us, and as wicked as we are, **we owe Him** that much. After all, if it had not been for His **creation of** the world of **human life** along with His Grace, you wouldn't even be here today. That is your **Father**; so **glorify His name** just as He does for you, even though you don't deserve it. Remember, when things don't seem to go right in your life, that is not ***God*** taking anything away from you, but it is ***Satan*** that causes you to lose out simply because you allow him to. I just wanted to shed some light on how we all go through storms, and it's just to make us stronger for the next one, because another one will come to help keep you focused on your ***faith***. If you want to live a happy and prosperous life so you can be a blessing to someone else, we **have** to live our life based on our **faith in God's Word.** It took for me to go through all of this for me to understand how important it is for me to **put God first** in my life. **Love God with** all of your **heart**, **mind**, **body**, and **soul**. **God works** with your heart, and **Satan works** with your mind. If you **follow your heart**, it will **take over your mind**.

Chapter 16:
Something Real

What is a real man? A real man stands for everything he speaks. He will never deceive you. He's patient, dedicated, understanding, loving, gentle, caring, respectful, honest, romantic, loyal, and he will never let you down. What is a real woman? A real woman is everything a real man is. We can be "anything" we want to be when we put our minds to it. When a man and a woman come together, there is nothing they can't achieve through ***Christ***. They will be there to look out for each other. When one falls, the other will be right there to catch them. They will never let each other be without. They will keep each other's spirit up and not disappoint one another. They will accept each other for who they are, and not try to change the other. Everything one does should almost always be satisfying to the other. I say "almost" because we know it is difficult to totally satisfy someone in today's society. That couple will **create a bond** that is so strong that it cannot be broken by anyone other than ***God***. They will create a love that is so strong, only ***God*** can change it. A love that never has to **say "I'm sorry,"** for the phrase alone speaks for itself. They will do whatever it takes to keep the other one happy. This is a love that can stand the test of time when they have each other's back. It's a special kind of love for unity through ***Christ***. This kind of love allows one to feel the pain, sadness, and joy of the other one when they are not together. When you have something or someone like this, it keeps your heart happy and an everlasting smile on your face. These are characteristics of Jesus, and He is in us, so it's not hard for us to adapt to this type of lifestyle. All you have to do is **let Jesus lead the way** and follow His path for your life. These kinds of feelings can only create "something real." Soul mates sent from **God**. With so much going on out here today, if we just had more **real** men and women, this would be a better world. We would all be out looking for the same results; peace and happiness. It is too bad and so sad that people are never satisfied with "just each other." It is not that hard to be satisfied with just enough! ***God*** wants us all to be happy and pleased, not disappointed and teased. He wants to give us everything our hearts desire. **Love is real** and serious. If you have it in you, which it is a ***God*** given gift, you would never use it to do another wrong or bring them any harm, nor cause them any pain. What makes things so difficult for people to do each other right? Everyone is out for themselves instead of for each other. They focus on how they can get someone to do something for "them," regardless of how it makes another person feel. They will step on and walk all over someone's heart, while taking advantage of their kindness, just to get what they want. They are only out to please their own wants and needs and other people around them who share the same evil characteristics. They have an "**I don't care attitude**." They always have to make someone feel worst than what someone else did; instead of dissolving things and making the situations better just as they wanted at one point in their life. There are many people out here today who just want to be treated right with love and respect and will do just about anything to get it, but it shouldn't have to be that way. **Be real** and honest with each other. If there is something or someone keeping you from totally or truly getting involved with someone the way you may want to, let that person know the real deal up front, and allow that person to make their own decisions on whether they choose to stay or go. Don't make that decision for them. We also have to recognize when ***God*** is trying to remove something from our lives. When you just feel like you are the only one putting your all into a relationship, it's time to accept the fact that, this is not the person you are meant to spend the rest of your life with. Sometimes you have to let things go in order for ***God*** to send the right person to you. If you are still clinging on to the one who is not for you, how will you ever accept the one who is sent to you? It's time to do right by each other. Don't just want to **be something** real; be **someone real**.

God is your best and true friend who will never leave you, never disappoint you, never mistreat you, never give up on you, never judge you, never stop loving you; instead He will always listen to you, He will always be right by your side and He will never talk about you to anyone else or behind your back. These evil and mean things are what we do to ourselves and let others do to us. ***God*** doesn't play a part in evil. We need to be more of a true friend to each other and stop mistreating people. Be a friend who is truthful, faithful, loving and honest even if it hurts, but do it in a ***Christian way***. Real friends always look out for each other. Real friends cry and laugh together while feeling each other's pain. Don't be the kind of friend who will sit back and watch someone you claim to be a friend to prepare themselves for something disastrous, painful, harmful or regretful just to keep them from being upset with you. They may be set in their ways, but that should not be an excuse for not intervening on their behalf to try and stop them. Even though you may have spoken to them about the same issue before, keep pushing because one day they will see that you care and thank you for not giving up on them throughout their many failures. When they fall, you should be right there to pick them up, not keep them down. Hug them and let them know everything is going to be alright. The way through to a friend is not by being a harsh, forceful or a pushover, but by showing love and support. The way you come at that friend and the way you use your words is what makes the difference in how you make that friend feel about how the result ends. It's the difference in what they see as far as you being there to help or criticize and dictate their moves in their life. On the other hand, that friend has to appreciate a true friend for trying to help and being there to support. We need to understand and realize that a real friend is the only one who is going to speak about something they see wrong only because they care. We need to learn to be more appreciative toward our friends and deal with the constructive criticism and advice. After all, they are the ones looking in from the outside, and they are the ones with the better view. We give advice to each other because of personal experiences of our own or someone else's. Either way it is helpful and beneficial if we just listen. We need to recognize that these friends are in our lives for a reason, and being that we choose to keep them around, we should value their opinions and advice without thinking there is some kind of ulterior motive for helping or looking out for our best interest. True friends are hard to come by so keep the ones you have and find other people to be one to. Be a true friend that is more like ***Christ*** and one who can be trusted with someone's life. Don't just be something real, but be someone real.

Chapter 17:
Stop Complaining

Why do we complain so much? Why do we always want everything to fit our needs and our own world? Why is it so hard for us to adapt to change? What don't we understand about modern technology that causes things to change around us on a daily basis? Why is it that we can find every possible solution to everyone else's problems, but we can't find just "one" to our own? What makes our needs so much more important or special than the next individual's needs? We need to take more time to be more understanding and considerate to other people's situations and feelings, especially when we can't even understand our own. We need to be more mindful to the fact that not everything in life will suit our needs, so why should it be made perfectly for you? If it did work that way, we wouldn't have so many reasons to make complaints. I feel we need to take more time to evaluate the reasons of why we complain. If you just take the time out to observe and re-evaluate the changes made and accept the fact that most changes are being made to upgrade our situations, then we can find a way to positively apply these changes to our lifestyles. I can say from personal experience through my history of employment that I am ***trying my best*** to **stop complaining**, especially after listening to other people do it everyday. Complaining shows a sense of ungratefulness and lack of happiness. I am a Customer Service Associate working in a call center for a bank. Answering them phones and dealing with clients' attitudes and listening to their complaints is enough do drive you crazy **if** you let it. They complain about the issues they bring upon themselves. It's funny how no one likes to accept responsibility for their own actions. They complain about the smallest details. They talk to you any kind of way because you don't have the ability or authority to clean up their own mistakes. They complain about things that they have opportunity to change. They complain about having to pay for a call to speak with an associate, but yet and still they don't trust viewing their information online, and they won't listen to the options long enough to get their information through the automated system. They get mad because they get overdraft fees for just a couple of pennies, but they refuse to keep a record of their own transactions.

They don't like to wait for a long period of time on the line just to get their balance, but they hold anyway. They don't want to listen to options in Spanish. They don't like the type of account they have. They call you out your name and tell you how worthless and helpless you are, while throwing around their demands. If just for once, they would sit back and take some time to go over the things that they are not satisfied with and ask how they can make the situation different or better, they would feel a lot better and see just how much control they really have over there own situations. You don't have control over your life, but you can control what contributes to the outcome of your situation. You can adjust "any" situation to make it fit your needs if you just take out some time instead of taking out attitude. That would be too much like right because it would involve someone having to do their own work. We are so caught up in wanting someone else to do our work for us, and we wonder why and how someone can take advantage of us. We leave ourselves wide open for opportunity for someone's benefit by putting our trust in man. People don't realize that "man" looks for this opportunity to benefit from our mistakes. We can't put blame on anyone else but ourselves when we are in these predicaments.

I have done customer service for more than ten years now, and I have learned to just let the customer's speak on their feelings and opinions because they don't know me, and most of them just need to vent out their frustrations as well as looking for someone else to blame. I understand most of their issues because I have been in some of the same situations before with some of the same attitudes, so I don't take it personally. I have learned to put myself on the other side of the phone when they call in. They don't know much about the business I work for, so they won't understand it like I do. As a customer service associate, it is my job to help resolve the issues caused by the company I work for. Although I know I'm not responsible, I do work for the company, so I have to find a way to resolve the issue. It is kind of hard to sit back and listen to people degrade you and assault you with mean and nasty words, but that only let's me know just how lonely and miserable they are. I wonder if they ever realize that the way they treat people is part of the reason for the misery in their life. They can't harm me with their words; they don't even know me. For me to take anything they say personally, would mean that they are right about whatever they are saying. Although the calls are "***job***

security" for me, there are other options they have other than going about things they way they do. They just have to have everything go their way so their life can be made easier. They don't understand that maybe they had to wait on the line because there was someone before them who called and did the same thing. That is wasted time speaking on an issue that you know is not going to be resolved just because you yell and scream about it. Instead of asking their question, they rant and rave about their experience with the wait time. They wait for the same reason the next person has to wait. We are listening to their complaints instead of their problems so we can work on getting it resolved. I love being a Customer Service Associate because it gives me the opportunity to help others by giving them good advice so they can keep track of their own information. I can also give them other options to either help them to eliminate some of their issues or add onto some of their benefits. Anything I can do to put a smile on someone's face or in their heart is **a blessing for me** in itself. I pray just about every morning to be a blessing in this manner. I am honored and pleased to be a blessing however it may come. Even though I can't be a blessing the way "I" would like to, it makes me feel good just to know that I am one for however it may work out. I love for people to let me know how I made them feel good or special, because I know they see the light of ***Christ*** in me, and ***God*** gets all the glory from my actions. Like they say, "your actions speak louder than your words." You can "say" whatever you want to say about how good of a person you choose to be and how you like to help others, or how you do this and that, but if you don't live up to those words, they are meaningless. If we just take our time and go with the flow of the changing of times, we will be a lot better off with life. Allow yourself to accept the fact that the world is rapidly changing while technology is steadily moving up on a consistent basis. It's kind of like, "here today gone tomorrow." If we just take the time to read the information that is provided to us, we would spare ourselves a lot of headache and aggravation. Each of us pray and **ask God** to bless us with different things we may want or need. Most of us should be praying for patience and understanding. **God will bless you**, but He will only do it according to how you live your life. Just like things have to be perfect for you before you will do something for someone else, ***God*** will make sure that you are in the right Spirit and headed down the right path before helping you. Do you have enough patience and understanding to wait for the blessing to come to you? Do you still continue to get upset when ***God*** doesn’t move fast enough for you? Try something different. **Try Jesus**! He doesn't need your help, but you do need His. He did what He was sent to do, and now it is your turn.

Chapter 18: My Inspirations

I'm so am thankful and grateful for the many Pastors out here that are seriously preaching the **Word of God,** and how important it is for us to get our relationship right with ***Christ.*** I've been inspired by quite a few, starting with the ***Pastors*** that I've personally spent time with. There were only two I've been a sheep of, and that was Pastor Delano R. Paige of Pittsburgh, PA and Pastor Tommy D. King of Hope Mills, NC whose wing I am still under. Out of these two Pastors, I can honestly say that they are very serious and dedicated to what they preach and teach. There were many other inspiring Guest Pastors who came to our Church, whose names I don't remember, "**Forgive me Lord**," but they have moved me as well. There are others that I haven't personally met that I've watched on television like, G.E. Patterson, "**God** rest his soul," Joel Osteen, Creflo Dollar, Bernard Johnson, Paula White, Marvin Sapp and Donnie McKlurkin. **God sent** them to me in a magnificent way. When I would turn on my television set, it was always set on the right channel, and it didn't matter what time of the day it was, they were right there feeding me **God's Word** about the issues in my life at hand and how to resolve them. **God is** a good ***God*** and **always on time**. My issues I was going through were also resolved through ***gospel ministries*** that I would listen to in my car while driving to work. There were many artists that moved and inspired me. Just to name a few that kept me going on the road, there was Yolanda Adams, "This battle is not yours," "I've got the Victory," and "Someone's watching over you." Kirk Franklin and TD Jakes, "911," and Marvin Sapp's "I believe." My heart song is by Todd Curry and Focus, "**Jesus will fix it for you**." These few along with the Wow Gospel 2007 have really helped me through my pain, but my heart song is what drove me to strive for more in ***Christ*** and gave me relief to know that everything was going to be alright. I've also been inspired by ***Christian friends*** and associates that I'm around or talk to on the phone personally. One of my closest and dearest friends, Danielle Roberts whom I've just discovered to be a best friend to me ***in Christ,*** has helped me and lifted up my Spirits just by talking to her on the phone. We didn't keep in touch as much when I was in Pittsburgh, but once I left, she was the only ***friend*** that I could talk to about ***God*** and the things that I was going through. She gave me some good advice without judging me because she understood me. She was real with me in a way that she never made me feel bad about anything I did. She made me feel so comfortable because I knew I could talk to her about anything. I also had an associate at work name Tamika "Zelda" Smith who was an inspiration when I would come to work. Although no one ever really knew that I was having some very difficult situations, because I didn't display my problems at work, I would help lift other people's Spirit. I don't believe in taking your problems to work. You leave your problems at the door, and **if** you feel the need to pick them back up when you leave, then that's when you do so. When I would come to work, Zelda would correct me from doubting the things that ***God*** would do for me. She would always tell me "it's already done; you claim it and stop saying when and if it happens." That really gave me courage and strength to believe what my **God will** do for me. My sister Monica Long, my grandmother Christine Fields, and one of my daughter's godmother Diane Alexander all came to me at one of the most trying times in my life. They brought me through without them even knowing it. They came here to North Carolina and spent some time with me and my children. While they were here, we sat down and talked about the Bible and different experiences we had that has changed our ways of thinking as well as the way we do things. We spent late hours of the night just talking about ***Christ***, and it felt so good to have them around because they were lifting my Spirits so high off the ground. They don't know it, but they are a big part of the reason I am speaking here today. If ***God*** didn't send them to me, I don't know where I would be today. ***God*** is amazing and wonderful for how He works things out without our help. You only see the results as being amazing, when you let Him do what He loves to do for you. **I thank God** for those moments because I am so much stronger than I have ever been in my life. I can get past just about anything, because I know that we must go through a test to make sure we are where we are supposed to be as ***Christians***. I know I can **call on Jesus** and He will fix it all. He will send the right ***Spirit*** to you when you need a healing or miracle, but you must be in the right Spirit to recognize that they are **God sent**. My mother, Brenda Dirl, is my biggest inspiration who gives me strength just by watching her make it through all of her struggles since her teenage years. Her many struggles that she has endured is what keeps me going from day to day. She has been through so much more than I could ever imagine anyone to be able to bear, and she is still smiling and making her way through this world. She has lost her oldest and her youngest child, and she still finds enough strength to love the rest of her children as though we are all still around. She may not be going as strong as she would like, but just for me to see that she gets up every morning and do what has to be done is enough to let me know that if she can do it and I haven't gone through half of what she has been through, then I know I can do it. My mother is my hero and I love her to death. I Thank ***God*** for giving me to her, and I thank her for taking on the responsibility she created without giving me away.

To all of these Angels that have given me inspiration and remain to be in my life in some form, shape or matter; I just want you to know that I am so grateful and thankful for you being in my life. You allowed ***God*** to use you to bring me up when I was down. Even though you didn't know it because I didn't show it, you still remain to be a blessing in my life. As they say, "when you are down to nothing, **God** is up to something and that something **is always good**. I love you with all of my heart and soul and that will never change. I don't want any of my other friends and family to feel that I have left them out intentionally, but those whom I have spoken about have been given this special acknowledgment because this is all about me and my **walk with Christ** and His works that pulled me through. They were there for me "**spiritually**," but I do thank you also for being a part of my life. You have played your part for which ***God*** has brought us together to help me with some of my life's experiences. You were there for a reason and whether it was for me or for you, we were in each other's life. No one is excluded from my love. To my sister Chantel Brown, you are very special to me as well, and my prayer to you is that you find your strength from this book and it helps you build up your ***faith*** enough to trust in ***God*** alone. I'm not here speaking to you because I'm attempting or claiming to be a minister, nor I am trying to be better than anyone, but I'm doing what ***God*** has led me to do. I don't know what ***God*** has in store for me, but I feel good about doing this, and whatever it is He is preparing me for, I want to be ready. This book didn't start out to be this long, but once I sat down and starting writing and typing, my fingers just started pouring out everything that was in my heart. Everything that is in my heart is what ***God*** put there for me to express, and I have no problem with telling it like it is because this is not of me, but of the ***ONE*** in charge over our lives. It is amazing to how ***God*** uses us to do His work when we let Him use us. As I was proofreading this, there were so many things said in this book that has touched my heart to the core. There were things I couldn't even begin to imagine myself speaking on, but I realized that this was not of me, but the ***Holy Spirit*** in me that wanted and needed to be heard. I just wanted to let you in on the love that I felt coming from **inspirations** that **God** has **sent to minister** to me through His dedicated Servants. I appreciate them very much for allowing ***God*** to use them; otherwise I don't know where I would be or what I would be doing at this moment. I have turned my life around for the good. **I'm all about God's business** whether I'm solo or not. I am serious about what I am doing, and I'm looking for others who don't mind **being sold out for Christ**.

Chapter 19:
God Is The Answer

It should bother us to know that **we are God's children** and we won't do enough to stand up and represent His love for us. All **He wants** is for **us to be happy**. He even gave up His Son to prove to us just how much He truly loves us. **He gave Jesus** the power **to** reveal His existence to **us**, and all the wonderful things He can do for us. That still doesn't mean anything to us, **we** would rather **team up with Satan** and join forces with the world to set out for destruction, and we wonder why nothing ever seems to stay "right" in our lives. This is why we are always only temporarily happy. ***Christ*** is a love magnet. He brings all good things to you. We can't have it like this until we change our lives and fully accept ***Christ*** into our hearts and follow ***Jesus***. You can't be a ***Christian*** today and worldly tomorrow. Don't put off your decision to **live for Christ**, because you are not promised the next second. Make sure that you choose wisely because your decision is based on you going to **Heaven or Hell**. Choose today to live for yourself and not for others. No onc other than you can get you into Heaven no matter how many people pray for you. It's either one or the other. You are the one who can make a choice of how you live your life and how it will end. Just remember that the end of your life is a result of your past. Yes, we will sin, but your sins should not by using and mistreating other people in any form, shape, or matter. ***Christians*** are not supposed to stoop down to people's level when they get upset with us. Just because that individual feels like letting ***Satan*** take over their actions at that moment, doesn't mean we have to do the same thing. We are to represent Christ at all times with no excuses. If we hold and stand firm on **God's Ten Commandments**, we have just cut out 95% of our evil and sinful ways. **God blesses us**, but sometimes He stops for us to recognize the blessings that we have already received. We get so many blessings that we don't even consider as being blessings, so we take them for granted without ***giving thanks***. Our blessings come in many different forms. Our blessings are not always financially. They come through people when they are sent to us to help us resolve a problem; we just have to learn to recognize that fact. ***All blessings*** come from the human flesh that chooses to activate their ***Holy***

Spirit. ***God will*** bless us, but after a while He wants you to show what we are doing for Him. He wants to see that we really appreciate the things that He is doing for us and through us. Our gratitude is what helps us to elevate to the next level. He's not going to keep blessing us while we still walk, talk, and look the same. He wants us to **be sold (soul) out** for Him like we are for everything else. He wants to see if we will share the knowledge and wisdom He has given to us. He wants to know that we **have "faith"** in Him, and that we ***trust*** and ***believe*** He will do what we ask Him to do. If He says He will, there is nothing but all ***truth*** to that. He knows your heart's desires, your wants, and your needs. Your needs are always met without hesitation. Your wants and desires come with discipline, obedience and dedication to your ***Heavenly Father***. When you work for Him, He is more than pleased to work for you when you call. He does exactly what we do to people all over the world. When they show us they are deserving of something, or we feel we can trust someone with our things, and when we see them as being a good person, isn't that when we open our doors to them? So why should it **be** any different **with God**? **God is the way**; **God is the answer**. In everything you do, **apply** His **wisdom** and **knowledge**, it **adds details** to the goodness in your life.

If you are truly anointed and gifted with a talent and you recognize that it's a gift from ***God***, then you would never turn you back on someone being sent to you. With your gift, you should **have** enough **faith** and **belief** to know that **God** has given you the strength to overcome all. You should be able to help just about anyone in any situation. If you ***believe*** that someone approaching you or reaching out to you is sent from Satan, then where does your power of ***faith*** lie that allows you to **believe that you can** change this person's perspective **with God's help and your faith**? **God has the power** to change "all," circumstances. He has not been able to rest ever since evil came into the world. That is why **He is God** and you are you. Although some may feel differently, the truth can be confirmed by the asking yourself this question; "how can He rest if we call upon Him twenty-four hours and seven days of the week, which is **365 days** of the year?" There are miracles being performed on a daily basis throughout this world from so much madness and tragedy. **God works 24\7**, so we should never be unavailable to help someone when they come to us, because He is in us and works through us. We may become doctors and nurses to heal the sick, but it is ***God*** who is using your hands to do the performance for the healing process. The only power we have in us is the power that ***God*** has given to Jesus, who lives in us, and it is only activated through our ***faith*** in what we do. When your prayers go up to **ask for God's help** so you can do a successful job in what you are doing, that is ***Jesus*** calling out to His Father on your behalf to work for you and through you so that **God will** be glorified by your success. I made that statement that way so that we will get in the habit of learning to **put God first** by asking how He can be glorified from our actions before we do something. We may be judges and lawyers to help people stay out of jail, but it is ***God*** who opens your eyes to the truth. ***God*** uses the human body to work His miracles for us so that He may be ***glorified***. There is nothing done in this world today without the works of the ***Lord***, but for some reason we trip on the belief that we do these things ourselves. We were not born with all this knowledge, but it is everywhere for us to learn about it. There shouldn't be a time of the day where we can't set aside some time and do what we are asked to do whether it be from ***God*** or someone else in this world. It doesn't matter if you're eating, bathing, sleeping, or just resting. You should always be there just as we expect ***God*** to be. You never know what that person is truly going through or dealing with, so you should always be ready to be a blessing in someone's life. This could be one of your **tests of dedication** to your **service for the Lord**. This life is not a chess game, and ***God*** does not use you as a "pawn." We don't need skills to master this life, just dedication and ***faith***. He created and equipped us so we could be more like Him with the power to lift the lost out of their dungeons of sin. **God is for us** not against us. He wants us to be and have the best. We don't feel that way for each other, so who is out for whom? If **you are a servant of God**, then **be the best** and take your job seriously ***for "Christ's Sake***!" It's time to do what **God** has **called us** to do. Don't let your opportunity pass by. We are not responsible for other people's actions, but we are responsible for our own. If you want someone to follow you, be a leader of Christ. Lead them into something positive. If we don't **choose God now**, after the age of twelve, we are "all" going to be judged for "everything" we do. ***God*** is the truth, the way and the only true “light” throughout this dark world.

Chapter 20:
When God Calls, Answer

The next time ***God*** calls you, don't go get permission from someone else; you move. He has already equipped you with necessities and direction to do what He has called you to do, so it would be in your best interest to respond instantly. One day you're going to need Him for an emergency and you're going to get that busy signal you're always giving Him. When you feel it, don't question it but do stand on it, act on it, and then begin to live it. Each of us is given a different vision and different insight about the talents and gifts we have, but they should all send out the same message. **We need God** more than He needs us. He can let this whole world go straight to Hell. Let's start to be better servants of ***God***. Let's be more true to ***God's Word***. He has a purpose for all of our lives, and it is time that we all find out what it is. Each and every one of us is set to play a part in everyone's life, and it is not to be evil or cause mental or physical pain. The goodness is in your heart, so go with the flow. Everything is not going to be what we expect, but it will be for the best. The only way you can have life the way you want it is to get in **touch with your spiritual side**, **read your Bible,** and **talk to God**. Yes, He knows you inside and out, but He knows more of what's in your heart, so let Him know what's on your mind. Reveal your true self to ***God***, and He will reveal the Truth to you. It costs nothing to learn and **hear the Word of God**, but it costs "you" everything when you don't **know the Word**. In case you didn't know, **Jesus is the Word**, so you may want to get to know Him before your time is up. Today should be the day for you. Oh, I forgot to ask, **how much time do you have** to get it right? Do you have another second, another minute, another hour, another month, or another year? Time is wasting, so come and join the forces and be a part of helping to stop the violence and evil by spreading ***the Word***. **Jesus Loves You**! We don't need anyone's permission to **do God's work**. He created us to do the work, and it pays more than what anyone's bank account holds and is better than any other offer anyone can ever make. **When God calls**, make sure **you Answer**. **Our reward** is hearing **those 3 words** when we reach the end of our journey and make it home, "**Job Well Done**."

When you decide that you are going to **answer the call**, please make sure it is truly **in your heart** and you are ready to give up your "worldly freedom." That means to be prepared to change "everything" in your life to make a change for the good. Be sincere at heart and stand firm when you make a decision to serve the Lord. When you accept a title under ***God***, you are representing the Father, so that means you have to change the way you think and how you treat people. You must **become** and handle your situations more **Christ-like**. ***Jesus*** was not a quitter, so why would you want to be one? You can't represent ***Christ*** when you are not true about what you are doing. How can you accept a title and then step down from it? How can you be certain that **God** has **called you** to do a certain ministry one day and the next day you are not sure? Maybe it was because you were not accepting this calling from ***God***, but from an evil spirit who wanted you to turn people away due to the things you would be representing. People will not see the light in you, but they will see the darkness all around you, and then eventually someone else's light will shine on you and uncover all of your secrets. ***Satan*** has won again, and now you turn other people away from believing that ***God*** can and will do anything. If they don't see your strength, what will give them hope that **God will strengthen** them? You know at the time you are answering the call that you have to be "willing" to **give up** everything "**evil**" in your life. You have to turn away from the "old" and get with the "new." I truly believe it is because that calling was never in your heart and the benefit was for self gain for ***Satan***. Regardless of how tough things may get in your life, you have to stick it out and **trust in God** to turn it around for you. The decision to accept the calling on your life was "your" ***choice***. Nobody "made" you do this. If you can preach and teach someone about how ***God*** operates off of their "***faith***," how do you show others what **God will** do for you if they don't **see your** trust and your **faith**? This is not for everybody, but just for those to whom it applies. When you answer the call, **God uses you** to be an example of how **His love works** for us. You are equipped with all of the wisdom and knowledge that you need, and when you start speaking, everything will pour out from your heart and give you understanding. At that time, it is no longer you doing the talking, but the ***Holy Spirit*** in you because you have allowed ***God*** to use you. When you doubt yourself about your calling or service for

God; you doubt His power and love for you. When you step down from a title, not only do you show how weak you truly are in spirit, but you can destroy other people's trust and belief by giving them the impression that if you can't do it and you were ***in Christ***, then how can they. Why would they want to get to know someone they feel will be of no benefit to them? You are destroying people's "**Faith**." Your job is to be more like "**Christ**" and **save**, not like **Satan** and **destroy**. You are to be that example of the strength that ***God*** gives when you stay focused on ***His promises***. We know He will never leave us and He will "always" pick us up when we fall in His name. If you are a true child of ***God*** doing His works and you truly let Him take care of you, and you **have** complete and total "**faith**" in Him, then you know that the test you are going through is for others to see how He works when He brings you through. How can we be a testimony to His promises if we are not dedicated to our services for Him?

Stop playing and pretending to be ***Christians*** while making excuses to do wrong. There is no excuse, so let's stop using them. We have the will power to stop doing "anything" we "want" to, and if we put **God** first in our lives, we can accomplish any goal we set. Just like we set our minds to achieve goals for an education for our careers so we can buy that dream car or that house we want, we need to set our minds to being dedicated to **the One and Only** who makes these things possible for us. If you believe you achieve these things by yourself because you deserve them, then you are more lost than you think. If you are choosing to live for the moment each day, then make it about doing something that will make a difference for more than just yourself. When you leave here, what kind of impact will you leave with the world? Will there be good things spoken about you and the many things you've done for other people? Will they say you were a good person and fun loving to be around? Will they speak about the light you let shine from your smile when you would come into the room? Will people speak about how you have touched them in so many ways? Will they say you were the type of person that would give someone the shirt off of your back? Will they say you would always try to make peace with others? Will they say you were always eager to help someone, especially someone who couldn't help themselves? Will they say you had a good heart? Will your eulogy be filled with good memories of fun and laughter, or will the majority of the people you have come in contact with be glad that you are gone and out of the way? The life you choose to live is very important to your present and your future, so please choose wisely. ***Satan*** has already reserved a spot for you in his world of ***Hell***. You can call and change that reservation for Heaven. ***God*** is calling and reaching out to you. He is pouring His heart out to you about the pain you are causing Him by allowing ***Satan*** to take over your mind and enter your heart. Don't let your mind take over what should matter to you the most; your life. **Give your life to Christ** and don't let ***Satan*** get it, because he is going to take it straight to ***Hell*** with him. **God loves you** more than you can ever imagine and more than you want to believe. Don't let "anyone" tell you otherwise. He wants you to call on Him and make your reservation for His ***Hallelujah Harvest***. **Be more serious about God**, and instead of jumping into what "you" want to do, allow Him to change, prepare and lead you to what He is calling you to do. If you just open up your heart and receive Him, **God will** work on you to get you to where you need to be so you can handle your position. When you are serious about your service for the ***Lord***, everyone you come in contact with should notice and comment on how "there is something different about you that they just can't put their finger on." They should always feel blessed just to be around you. That is not being big-headed or making it seem like you are better than anyone, that is just a reward of peace and joy for your obedience, and it shows that you are doing what you are supposed to do. He loves you and only wants the best for you. **Have Faith in God** and let Him lead the way. Remember that "**without**" **Him you are nothing**, but "**with**" **Him, you are everything. Without** "**faith**" **you have nothing**.

Chapter 21:
What Is Faith?

Are you a ***faithful*** servant? Faithful means to be ***full of faith***. Can you say that you **have faith in the Lord**? Can you go on about your business without a worry in the world, outside of tragedy, "knowing" that everything will be alright? Do you truly **trust in God** to do as He says? When you **pray to God**, do you pray **in the name of Jesus**? Do you really know what ***faith*** means and what it is? ***Faith*** is a firm belief in something for which there is no proof; without having doubt. Your ***faith*** is what "allows" you to trust and believe that ***God*** is going to **answer** your ***prayers***. Praying in ***faith*** is when you "see" no possible way to get through a circumstance but through ***God***. When nothing about that circumstance seems to go your way and you are about to go over the edge, that's when you **activate your faith** and **show God** that you trust Him without a shadow of doubt. Your blessings manifested through your ***faith*** will **give God the Glory** for everyone to see so they will want to do the same. **God deserves "all" the Glory** because He is the one ***giving*** you something amazing just by making a call out in His Son's name. This can't happen until someone becomes an example of His love by standing for what they believe in. When all looks gloomy and the smoke is too thick, that's when you **call on God** to perform a miracle in your life to help change the circumstance for the better. A ***miracle*** is an extraordinary event manifesting divine intervention in human affairs; something unusual. ***God*** will perform a miracle in your life to get you through, but how can it be a miracle if you don't believe in your ***faith***? If you learn nothing else out of this, believe that the only way **God will** even **acknowledge your faith** in Him, is through His Son ***Jesus***. You "must" **know Jesus** before you can even call out to ***God***. ***Jesus*** is the spirit in you, and His spirit must be activated at "all" times in order for ***God*** to hear you. That is why is it extremely important for us to **get to know Jesus** so He can change our hearts and renew our lives. When you change, it starts with the heart. Once you come to know Him, your walk will change, the way you talk will change, the way you love will change, and the way you treat others will change. It's never too late for change. There are testimonies of "***faithful***" servants written in ***the Bible***. Daniel was put in a lion's den and came out untouched, and his friends were put into a burning furnace and came out burn and smoke free. Not one piece or stitch of their clothing was burned, nor did it reek of smoke. That's the kind of faithful servant ***God*** is still looking for today. When ***God*** comes back, He is coming for what is His, and if He doesn't see His Son in you, don't even expect to see His arms open up for you. As a matter of "fact," you won't even know who He is when He comes back because you never took the time to find out what it would be like. **God tells us** that in the book of ***Revelations***. Revelation means to reveal or **uncover the truth**. ***God*** doesn't hide anything from us; we just have to seek the truth for ourselves. Take time and be more serious about what ***God*** is doing to and through you. We can all make a difference in this world, but it starts with "you" first. Step up and make a change. This is about ***God***, not you.

After everything that has been spoken and presented to you, I want you to ask yourself; "do I **have faith** and if so**, where is it**?" **Faith is the key factor** of your life. It is your blessings activated through prayer. **Without faith** your life is nothing. Without ***faith*** you will always fall short of the blessings that should be overflowing in your life. Your **faith** is what **activates God's power** over your life. ***God*** is waiting to bless you, but you don't truly believe in your heart without a shadow of doubt that He's going to do it the way you ask. **God will give** you anything you ask, and that is written in ***the Bible***. **God will** give you the very thing that you ask, but you have to know Him, live for Him, walk for Him, be willing to sacrifice your life for Him, and willing to do what He has called you to do. He won't move for you unless you move for Him. ***God*** doesn't require any real labor from us. His requirements for us are to love, trust and obey Him. There is nothing hard to do out of any of those requirements. To love someone doesn't even require movement. If you find that to be labor, that is because you are a "very" selfish person. ***Trust*** me; you will get nothing out of this life using those characteristics. Everything He asks of you is exactly what He has already done for us. I would like to introduce an example to you of how your ***faith*** will bring everything you pray for and have serious desires for that will come to past. I am going to use praying for a wife as an example, and I only use a wife because it is written in the Bible about "he" who finds a good thing finds a wife. If you pray for a wife and you are specific in what kind of woman you are looking for as far as being honest, faithful, dedicated, and full of love, especially when you are looking for one in ***Christ***, ***God*** will send you a woman with all of those characteristics. She may not be the most beautiful woman or have a "slamming" body, but she will give you the kind of love and dedication you want in your life. When ***God*** points her out to you, will you accept the one He gave you or pick your own? Will you question ***God*** or ask yourself is this real? Will you pass up that opportunity because she may not be "exactly" what you prayed for? Maybe something is off about the way she walks or the way she talks. Will you continue to second guess what you have prayed for? Is it unbelievable? Does it make you say this is too good to be true? Will you go back and remember all of the qualities you asked for? If you answer yes to only two of these questions you have already doubted your ***faith***. The reason you ask is because that's how **God works**. **Only God** can bring things to you just as you ask. **God puts you in the right place at the right time** and there is no mistake about it. The only way you will miss that blessing is if you don't have that live connection with ***God***, which means you have no ***faith***, so how would you know that you are being blessed? I just have one question for you. How long would it take for you to bring this answered prayer to past? When you have complete and total faith in ***God*** and what He can do for you, why would waste any time bringing it to reality? If ***God*** presented it to you, then He intended for it to be just the way you asked, so why would you wait? Would you be bold enough to stand up and show ***God's children*** what ***faith*** is all about or would you put it off on hold waiting for "your" time? This goes back to what I have been speaking about above of how **your faith activates your blessings**. If **God is in the mist** of everything you do and you truly believe, trust and **love the Lord** from the bottom of your heart, and you know without a shadow of doubt that He makes no mistakes, when you receive your blessings and you immediately act on them you can't go wrong. ***God*** will be there every step of the way to make sure that everything goes the way it was planned. What I'm about to say is based off of "***true faith***." When you meet this woman, you would take her and get married knowing that she is everything you wanted, so what could go wrong? ***God*** will set everything in motion for all to go as planned without worry just because He sees that you trust Him to do what He said. If you're not going to believe it when you get it, why even ask for it. Trust Him to lead the rest of the way, and "**never**" **question God**, yourself, or go out of your way to ask someone else about what you have prayed for when it is presented to you. None of us have real "***faith***" because we don't know what it truly means to have it. We can talk about it until we are blue in the face, but if it's not in our hearts to where we would question whether or not it's what ***God*** sent, it's not true ***faith***. You will only know that it is sent from ***God*** if you have that live connection with Him, and you trust and believe in Him without a shadow of doubt. Get connected and **put God first** in your life. He doesn't make mistakes we do. You will know if you are putting ***God*** first in life when you sit back and think about how much you think about Him. Ask yourself this one simple question; "if ***God*** was to think about me as much as I think about Him, how much time of the day would he spend thinking about me?" Would it be maybe five, ten fifteen, or even thirty minutes? Would it be half or most of the day? Where you are in Him is where He is in you.

Chapter 22:
"Who Am I?"

I am the image of the only "begotten **Son**," and because I am made of thee, that makes me **#1**.

Why should I think of myself any **less**? That's how I got in this **mess**.

When I look around I can see there is so much to **do**, so why should I accept a thought of being **#2**?

I was created with all kind of wisdom and knowledge, especially with **love**. This came from the One up **above**.

When I think of goodness, it always comes back to **Grace**. I think about how I can't wait to see His **face**.

I can be anything that I want to **be**, with a gift of many talents because He didn't limit **me**.

I strive and I try to do my very **best**, but after a while I see that it's just a **test**.

I have to stop and get a feel for what's in my **heart**. Now I know that Jesus was here from the **start**.

As a Spirit He dwells inside of **me,** giving me enough strength, courage, and inspiration to trust and **believe**.

To find out who I truly am I must look inside and **out**, and I shall see that I am a free, gentle, kind and loving spirit no **doubt**.

There's nothing better to be than one of God's **creations**. After all, we were born into His **nation**.

Now that I know who I am without a shadow of **doubt**, I am happy and satisfied to know what I'm all **about**.

Christ loves me and I love **Christ**, and for Him I will make a **sacrifice**.

I have to love me for whom I am, and that's the real **deal**, because I know if I don't, who else **will**?

I have to first love **myself**, before I can learn to love anyone **else**.

So when you come along and you ask "**who am I**," I won't have to tell you a **lie**.

These are just some messages that I would send out to my friends and family through text messaging just to start the day off. I would like to share them with you as well. Maybe you can share them with someone you know.

-It is your judgment day. Are you ready? Which way will your scale tip?
-Would you give up your child's life to save others?
-When you look in the mirror, do you see Christ or Satan? When you plan your day, do you plan to fail or triumph? When you think of the end, do you see Heaven or Hell?
-We don't need a co-signer, God is our Father & His Son Jesus has already signed for us.
-God, the Father, is the ruler of my world. His, Son Jesus, is the Head of my household, and the Holy Spirit lives in me.
-God gave up His Son for you, what will you give up for Him?
-There is an "invitation only" party coming up so make sure you get your invitation. You don't want to miss this party; it is the celebration of the return of Christ.
-God is looking for a faithful and dedicated friend. Is that you?
-God wants to introduce Himself to you. He's all that and more, so bring some friends when you come.
-God's love is unconditional; can you match that?
-God never left you and He has always been good to you, so why did you leave Him?
-Satan is on fire in Hell and God is on cloud nine in Heaven! How will you feel at the end of your journey?
-God gave you life; don't you think He should be good enough for your time?
-It's your choice, so choose your destiny wisely!
-God is going to give you what you gave Him. Will it be Hell?
-Jesus is going to stand up for you the same way you stood up for Him!
-God came to you as an enemy and the homeless, and you ignored Him and turned your back on Him. You still ask why your prayers don't get answered.
-How did you wake up this morning? You still believe it was your alarm clock? How were you able to hear it? God is in control of "everything!"

The significance between the **bold** text and the ***italic*** text is that the **bold** text emphasizes the importance of the sentence or paragraph, and what and who this is all about so you will never forget who you are and what you should be doing, and the ***italic*** text signifies Jesus' **purpose** and what we need to remember and do to overcome all the evil in this world. You may have noticed that a lot of this information was repetitious, but keep in mind that it is done that way so that you don't forget the purpose of this book. When you or anyone else around you picks up this book, the text in ***italic*** will be right there to remind you of what to do. If you would like to contact me, you can email me at tmhardwick1@yahoo.com or iamwhitted@bellsouth.net.

God bless every pair of eyes that has read this book. May it reach deep down in their souls and touch their hearts as they receive this opportunity to be motivated and more dedicated to you. May they feel your pain from all the wickedness in this world and want to be better servants to you and the purpose of your Son's death. Give them the strength to love and help each other more than ever before. Bless their homes and their families as they strive to become better servants for you. Father forgive us for our sins, change our hearts, and renew our minds in the name of Jesus I pray. **Amen.**

www.ingramcontent.com/pod-product-compliance
Lightning Source LLC
Chambersburg PA
CBHW032144040426
42449CB00005B/391
9780615203669